CHLOË MOSS

Chloë Moss's first play, *A Day in Dull Armour*, was produced by the Royal Court Theatre, London, for which she won the Young Writers Festival 2002.

Chloë was the Sheila Lemon Writer-in-Residence at The Bush Theatre in 2003-04 and Paines Plough in 2004.

Her play, *How Love Is Spelt*, premiered at The Bush in 2004. It was awarded a special commendation by the Susan Smith-Blackburn Award and received its US premiere at New York's Summer Play Festival in August 2005.

Chloë is under commission from Paines Plough, the Everyman Theatre, Liverpool, and the Royal Court.

Chloë Moss

CHRISTMAS IS MILES AWAY

NICK HERN BOOKS
London
www.nickhernbooks.co.uk

A Nick Hern Book

Christmas Is Miles Away first published in Great Britain
as a paperback original in 2005 by Nick Hern Books Limited,
14 Larden Road, London W3 7ST

Christmas Is Miles Away copyright © 2005 Chloë Moss

Chloë Moss has asserted her right to be identified as the author
of this work

Cover image: Claire McNamee

Typeset by Country Setting, Kingsdown, Kent CT14 8ES
Printed in Great Britain by Cox and Wyman Ltd, Reading, Berks

A CIP catalogue record for this book is available from
the British Library

ISBN-13   978 1 85459 908 7
ISBN-10   1 85459 908 9

Christmas Is Miles Away was first performed at The Studio, Royal Exchange Theatre, Manchester, on 2 November 2005, with the following cast:

CHRISTIE BENSON   David Judge
LUKE MICHAELS   Paul Stocker
JULIE BRIDGES   Georgia Taylor

Director   Sarah Frankcom
Designer   Jamie Todd
Lighting Designer   Richard Owen
Sound Designer   Pete Rice
Voice Coach   Mark Langley

Company Manager   Katie Vine
Stage Manager   Tracey Fleet
Deputy Stage Manager   Lynn Howard
Assistant Stage Manager   Beth Dibble

*Chloë Moss would like to thank Sarah Frankcom,
Sophie Marshall and everyone at the Royal Exchange,
Mel Kenyon, Graham Foulds, Georgia, Fudge and
Paul and Nick Bagnall*

CHRISTMAS IS MILES AWAY

For Phoebe-Chi

Characters

CHRISTIE BENSON, *sixteen to eighteen*

LUKE MICHAELS, *sixteen to eighteen*

JULIE BRIDGES, *sixteen to seventeen*

The action takes place in Manchester between February 1989 and October 1991.

– indicates an interruption.

. . . indicates the speaker trailing off or a change of thought.

This text went to press before the end of rehearsals and may differ from the play as performed.

Scene One

February 1989. Early evening. Boggart's Clough: a large parkland in Manchester. CHRISTIE and LUKE, both sixteen, are struggling to assemble a small two-man tent in their usual spot; a little patch by the lake, tucked away amongst overgrown bushes and shrubbery. LUKE is wearing a Lacoste knitted hat and a Berghaus jacket, CHRISTIE a black and red lumberjack's coat that is too big for him and a deerstalker hat. Their rucksacks are on the floor.

LUKE. You stupid?

CHRISTIE. What?

LUKE. It doesn't go like that . . . you feed it through the top, yer mong.

CHRISTIE. How many times have I done this?

LUKE. Exactly. Should know how to fuckin' do it by now . . . take yer gloves off'd be a start.

CHRISTIE. Fuck off.

CHRISTIE pulls one glove off and throws it on the floor.

I'll get frostbite.

LUKE. It's nearly March, yer big puff.

CHRISTIE. So, it's freezin' . . . I can't concentrate.

LUKE. Stop fuckin' daydreamin', be up in a minute if you paid attention.

CHRISTIE. I'm losing consciousness through hypothermia . . . not fuckin' daydreamin'.

LUKE. Yes yer are. Julie Bridges' legs wrapped round yer –

CHRISTIE. Shurrup.

LUKE. Through the fuckin' top . . . wake up, Christie, fuck's sake.

CHRISTIE. Do it yer fuckin' yerself then.

CHRISTIE *throws the pole down and sits down, head in hands.*

LUKE. Fuck's up wi' you?

CHRISTIE. Nothin'.

LUKE *carries on with the tent.*

She didn't say anythin'?

LUKE. No.

CHRISTIE. Nowt?

LUKE. I'm tellin' yer –

CHRISTIE. As if.

LUKE. She never –

CHRISTIE. Not a word?

LUKE. Nope. Pegs . . . get up will yer.

CHRISTIE *reaches for the bag of tent pegs from the floor, takes a handful, then passes the rest over to* LUKE. *They place the flysheet over and start securing it with the pegs.*

CHRISTIE. Just blanked yer?

LUKE. Yep.

CHRISTIE. What like . . . expression did she have?

LUKE. What d'yer mean?

CHRISTIE. On her face. Did she y'know . . . smirk or anything?

LUKE. I dunno, she was walkin' away. I couldn't see.

CHRISTIE. Did you just let her go?

LUKE. Course I fuckin' did. What did you want me to do, get her in a headlock?

CHRISTIE. She just carried on walkin' –

LUKE. Like she hadn't heard me.

CHRISTIE. She might be deaf.

LUKE. I've seen her talkin' to people . . . like normal.

CHRISTIE. She might lip-read.

LUKE. She might, yeah. Next time I see her, I'll let me airgun off right by her ear. If she doesn't jump then we can try somethin' else. Write on a bit of card.

CHRISTIE. It's not funny.

LUKE. You know she's not fuckin' deaf.

CHRISTIE. I wasn't serious.

LUKE. She might a' thought I was windin' her up. I don't know her. Never fuckin' spoke to her before. Only seen her 'round. Felt a bit of a dickhead actually, mate. But I did it. Fer you. Didn't I? Sorry it didn't come off like you wanted . . . happens sometimes. You'll get used to it.

The tent is up, they both stand back to look at it.

Couldn't swing a fuckin' midget in that, could yer?

Pause.

CHRISTIE. I'm not arsed anyway.

LUKE. Course you're not.

CHRISTIE. I'm not.

LUKE. S'alright. You're allowed.

CHRISTIE. I just . . . I don't believe yer.

LUKE. Yer what?

CHRISTIE. I don't believe yer but I'm not arsed.

LUKE. She didn't fuckin' say nothin' . . . why would I lie?

CHRISTIE. Protectin' me feelin's.

LUKE. Wha' the fuck would I wanna do that for?

LUKE *crawls into the tent.* CHRISTIE *sits outside for a moment, sulking, until he is aware of a noise – the wind rustling through the trees – and scuttles inside. They both lean on their elbows side by side, half out of the tent.* LUKE *starts emptying one of the rucksacks and dividing the contents between himself and* CHRISTIE*; lager, crisps, chocolate, a flask. He opens it, takes a swig and passes it to* CHRISTIE.

Tea.

CHRISTIE *holds the flask but doesn't drink.* LUKE *takes his hat off, he has a number two skinhead.*

CHRISTIE. What's tha' about?

LUKE. What?

CHRISTIE. Yer 'ead.

LUKE. What's it look like?

CHRISTIE. Thought you were growing it.

LUKE. I was . . . Dennis kept saying I looked like a girl. Got the clippers out last night when he wa' pissed. (*Beat.*) I like it.

CHRISTIE. Right.

LUKE. Right what?

CHRISTIE. Nothin' . . . right . . . I'm just sayin' right.

LUKE. It'll grow back anyway. If I want.

LUKE *puts his hat back on.*

CHRISTIE. So. Right. Just go on from the –

LUKE. Oh fer fuck's sake, Christie.

CHRISTIE. From the beginnin'. One last time. Go 'ead . . . yer by hers an' she's walkin' along . . . an' you say?

LUKE. . . .

CHRISTIE *takes a swig from the flask before spitting it out violently.*

CHRISTIE. What the fuck's in that?

LUKE. Vodka.

CHRISTIE. Yer don't put vodka in tea, knobhead.

LUKE. D'yer wanna know what I said to her or wha'?

CHRISTIE (*still spitting onto the grass*). Yeah.

LUKE. Right. Last fuckin' time. I go, 'Alright, Julie, how's it goin', girl. What yer up to?' She was with that Shelley, that girl with the weird lip in the year below us, toddlin' alongside her, like a little fuckin' . . . mouse or summat . . . and I went, er . . . I went, oh I dunno somethin' like . . . I can't remember exactly . . . but it wasn't nothin' important, just shit . . . just like leadin' into it you know like . . . what I was getting at. So it was blah-blah fuckin' . . . bollocks and then I said, 'I know someone who fancies you' and she goes, 'Who?' and I said . . . you, obviously like, and . . . she didn't say nothin'. Just like fucking silence. So I said, 'Would you go wi' him like?' and she didn't say nothing again. Just walked off. That fuckin' Shelley kid with her lip, all fuckin' starin' . . . squeakin' after her.

Pause.

CHRISTIE. Wha' d'yer reckon?

LUKE. 'Bout what?

CHRISTIE. That.

LUKE. Wha' about it?

CHRISTIE. It's bad that, innit?

Pause.

LUKE. Well, I don't think it's particularly fuckin' good, do you?

CHRISTIE. What do I do now?

LUKE. Ask her yerself.

CHRISTIE. Yer reckon?

LUKE. Yeah.

CHRISTIE. Honestly?

LUKE. Yeah.

CHRISTIE. Say what like?

LUKE. Fuck's sake . . . yer like her . . . does she wanna go out wi' yer?

CHRISTIE. Where to?

LUKE. Anywhere. The pub.

CHRISTIE. Are yer trying to be funny?

LUKE. Put a suit on.

CHRISTIE. I had a suit on last time.

LUKE. Yer dad's . . . he's about a foot taller than yer. Yer can borrow mine.

CHRISTIE. It's too risky . . . imagine that, gettin' the knock-back with a bird.

LUKE. Pictures.

CHRISTIE. You can't talk in the pictures.

LUKE. Exactly, yer nugget . . . That's the 'ole fuckin' point.

CHRISTIE. I wanna talk to her.

LUKE. Wha' about?

CHRISTIE. I dunno.

LUKE. Paintin' . . . art?

CHRISTIE. I might . . . Grow up, will yer.

LUKE. Are you havin' a laugh? Grow up yourself and stop bleatin' on about it. You're borin' . . . d'yer know that? Borin'. You'd go off her anyway. Soon enough. You'd get fed up.

CHRISTIE. No way.

LUKE. Definitely. Coupla weeks. You'd be bored. I used to be much more serious about things when I was, y'know . . . a bit less experienced. Once yer've been round the block a few times – an' I'm not knocking you 'ere, Christie – I'm just sayin', yer get a bit more . . . blousey about it.

CHRISTIE. Blasé.

LUKE. It's not love, mate . . . you don't love Julie fuckin' what's-her-face –

CHRISTIE. Bridges.

LUKE. Yer don't love Julie Bridges.

LUKE *takes the flask and gulps it back.*

CHRISTIE. What yer doin'?

LUKE. What's it look like?

CHRISTIE. We'll have nothing left, divvy.

LUKE. Yer've just spat it out.

CHRISTIE. It was the shock . . . could grow on me, I reckon. Least it's hot.

LUKE *passes it back,* CHRISTIE *takes the tiniest sip.*

LUKE. Don't go mad.

Pause.

How's yer dick?

CHRISTIE. Itchy.

LUKE. Still? Have yer been the doctor's?

CHRISTIE. You know I haven't . . . as if I'd go on me own.

LUKE. I keep sayin'. Make an appointment and I'll fuckin' come wi' yer –

CHRISTIE. The receptionist does aqua aerobics wi' me mam.

LUKE. There's nothin' wrong wi' yer anyway.

CHRISTIE. How do you fuckin' know?

LUKE. Cos you can't get Aids from a wank.

CHRISTIE. She had . . . sores on her hand.

LUKE. Louise Marsh. I told you, didn't I? You'd only regret it
. . . three months this has been goin' on. S'fuckin' ridiculous.
It's psycho – what d'yer call it?

CHRISTIE. Somatic. D'yer think so, yeah?

LUKE. I know so, mate.

CHRISTIE. Thanks, Luke. I know I think . . . I get meself
anxious. It's only cos –

LUKE. I know it. Shut it, yer mong.

Pause.

D'yer see that then?

CHRISTIE. What?

LUKE. There. That's a shootin' star, that, yer know.

CHRISTIE. S'a helicopter.

Pause.

LUKE. Oh aye yeah. I made a wish n'all.

CHRISTIE. What d'yer wish for?

LUKE. Doesn't matter now, does it? (*Beat.*) S'top, innit?
Outdoors.

CHRISTIE. Yeah.

LUKE. Massive.

CHRISTIE. I was born outdoors.

LUKE. Cos you're a tramp.

CHRISTIE. Fuck off –

LUKE. Joke. Tell us again.

CHRISTIE. No.

LUKE. Oh go on. Makes me laugh.

CHRISTIE. Me mum and dad went to a weddin' and I started
to come early . . . it was a knees-up in this hotel, this posh
place near Cheshire . . . in the night . . . so me dad just got

me mum in the car and Starsky-an'-Hutched-it to the hozzy
but it was too late cos me 'ead started to come out –

LUKE. Eeh . . . fuckin' gross –

CHRISTIE. So they stopped and the car was full of shit, me
mum said . . . maps and de-icer an' Sayers bags. So she got
out and laid on the grass at the side of this lane and by the
time the ambulance come, I was there. Born. Me mum says
she likes it that the first thing I saw was the sky and the stars.

LUKE. I was born in Stockport. General Hozzy. It's shit there.
Stinks of piss.

CHRISTIE. Me mum reckons it's important what you see first
. . . the very first thing in the world that you lay your eyes
on; that can be a big influence. She says I'm well lucky.

LUKE. She's a hippy your ma, isn't she?

CHRISTIE. No.

LUKE. Hippies are alright. Mods are better though. My dad
was a mod.

CHRISTIE. She's nothin' . . . she just thinks some things.

LUKE. Mods had better music. Mods were fuckin' well cool.
Once a mod, always a mod. Dennis had a scooter. He went
in big mad convoys to . . . all them places where the mods
went. Your dad wore a necklace, didn't he?

CHRISTIE. He never.

LUKE. He did . . . proper beads. Why you lying? It's on your
mum's dressing table.

CHRISTIE. What you doin' going in me mum's room anyway?

LUKE. To sniff her knickers.

CHRISTIE *grabs* LUKE, *getting him in a headlock.*

The door was open . . . fuck off.

CHRISTIE (*letting go*). Anyway, it wasn't a necklace like girls
wear. Everyone wore 'em in those days.

LUKE. My fuckin' dad never.

CHRISTIE. Give it up.

LUKE. Just sayin'.

CHRISTIE. Well, don't.

LUKE. S'not my fault yer bird's not interested.

CHRISTIE. Sometimes I forget why you're me best mate,
Luke. This is one of them sometimes.

LUKE. Cos you love it when I wind yer up . . . and I don't
take no notice of your sensitive side. Her problem, isn't it,
though, eh? Really. I know loads of girls fancy yer.

CHRISTIE. Who?

LUKE. I knew you'd do that. (*Thinks for some time.*) Andrea
Wise.

CHRISTIE. Johnno's sister?

LUKE. Yeah . . . can you not tell?

CHRISTIE. She's in first year.

LUKE. She fancies yer.

CHRISTIE. She's eleven.

LUKE. Yeah I'm not saying you'd wanna do owt about it . . .
but give her couple of years, say fourteen. Braces off.
Couple a' stone lighter. She's got a lovely little face.

CHRISTIE. You're weird.

LUKE. Says him.

CHRISTIE. Who else?

LUKE. Who else who?

CHRISTIE. All these girls.

LUKE. I'm too scared to say anyone else in case you take off
on me again.

CHRISTIE. If they're over eleven I don't mind.

LUKE. Me Auntie Barbara.

CHRISTIE. Fuck's sake –

LUKE. Reckons you're gonna be a stunner. She's only thirty-four.

CHRISTIE. Stone.

LUKE. Nice one. Cheeky cunt.

CHRISTIE. I don't care anyway. Don't want anyone to fancy me. Just Julie.

LUKE. You are never gonna get laid with attitude, lad.

CHRISTIE. Stop going on about it. It's only sex.

LUKE. That's what virgins say.

CHRISTIE. Luke –

LUKE. Joke. C'mon, I'm having a laugh with yer. No problems.

CHRISTIE. I'm not laughing.

LUKE. You never fucking are. Should try it.

        Pause.

CHRISTIE. I can't come away, yer know.

LUKE. Why not?

CHRISTIE. Me mum kicked off . . . I'd just go like, but she won't give me no money . . . she hasn't got any, she said.

LUKE. Yer just got a new kitchen.

CHRISTIE. That's what I said. But she said that's why she hasn't got any . . . cos of the kitchen.

LUKE. Fuckin' . . . so what are you sayin'?

CHRISTIE. Sorry –

LUKE. You're not comin' –

CHRISTIE. I really wanna come.

LUKE. But you're not.

CHRISTIE. What can I do?

LUKE. How long've you known you're not comin'?

CHRISTIE. Not long –

LUKE. When did yer ask yer mum? I bet it was ages ago –

CHRISTIE. Last week . . . I didn't wanna say –

LUKE. We've been talkin' about it all week.

CHRISTIE. I knew what yer . . . I didn't wanna say.

LUKE. Hippies aren't meant to be arsed about fitted kitchens.

CHRISTIE. She's not a hippy.

LUKE. Imagine no possessions an' all that.

CHRISTIE. Fuck off . . . What d'yer want me to do?

LUKE. Come away.

CHRISTIE. How?

LUKE. Just come away.

CHRISTIE. This is good though.

LUKE. What is?

CHRISTIE. This . . . here . . . it's good.

LUKE. Yeah it's good. So what? Been good since we were
    nine, other places are good too, y'know. I wanna go away.

CHRISTIE. Here's away.

LUKE. No it's not.

CHRISTIE. It is, it's –

LUKE. It takes us half an hour to get home . . . that isn't away,
    Christie. That's . . . here.

CHRISTIE. It's like the country . . . you just said though,
    didn't yer? You like it. This is enough I reckon . . . we could
    make it longer. Go fishin'.

LUKE. I don't fuckin' wanna come back . . . it's shit, why
    would I wanna come back here? Eh? When I was meant to

be going to Amsterdam? Eh? Amsterdam. Field down the road. Amsterdam. Field down the road.

Pause.

CHRISTIE. I haven't got any money.

LUKE. Well, get some . . . get a fuckin' job or somethin'.

CHRISTIE. I've got one.

LUKE. A paper round. Get a proper one . . . with money not fuckin' free bags o' Space Invaders and £1.50.

CHRISTIE. I haven't got time to . . . you know I haven't got time.

LUKE. Yer mam'd let you off . . . w'unt she? Sat'days? Like me.

CHRISTIE. For yer dad . . . getting double what anyone else'd get.

LUKE. Shurrup . . . I'm a grafter, me. Earn every penny.

CHRISTIE. There wouldn't be enough time even if I did. We're meant to be goin' in what? Three weeks? How'm I gonna get enough for Amsterdam in three weeks?

LUKE. You don't even wanna come.

CHRISTIE. You know I wanna come . . . I can't.

LUKE. You can do whatever you wanna do . . . if yer put yer mind to it. Dennis Michaels, 1983.

CHRISTIE. It does me head in, that.

LUKE. What?

CHRISTIE. You . . . quotin' yer dad all the time. Sayin' it like that. Everyone says that. He didn't make it up. It isn't deep or anythin'.

LUKE. I never said it was . . . who gives a shit about 'deep'? Deep's for hippies.

CHRISTIE. And you know what else does me head in?

LUKE. No an' I don't wanna. You bore the tits off me.

CHRISTIE. The way you never get into things that are happenin' now.

LUKE. Wharra you on about?

CHRISTIE. You said you liked the country before.

LUKE. It's alright . . . I do . . . it's alright like.

CHRISTIE. But like since we got here, all you've gone on about is being somewhere else, doin' somethin' else . . . the next thing. Goin' to Amsterdam. Somethin' better than this.

LUKE. So?

CHRISTIE. We're meant to be havin' a laugh.

LUKE. We are.

CHRISTIE. We're not now.

LUKE. That's your problem then.

CHRISTIE. No it isn't . . . it's you . . . makin' me feel . . .

LUKE. What?

CHRISTIE. I dunno. I can't relax.

LUKE. What. The fuck. Are you on about?

CHRISTIE. Sometimes. When I'm on me own with yer. I feel like I can't say what I want to. I just . . .

Pause.

LUKE. Go 'ead.

CHRISTIE. I mean . . . I meant like . . . all the things that I like you for . . . love . . . about yer –

LUKE. Watch it –

CHRISTIE. All the things that did or do make me wanna be your best mate . . . the way you're a cocky fucker but funny with it, and you won't hear no from no one or yer always up for it . . . stuff like that. And that yer dead sound about listenin' to me goin' on . . . I think about it more when it's just me and you and it's me you're bein' the big 'I am' with . . . and I think about the way I'm not like that and maybe that's why I like you cos you're not like me but I don't like yer doin' it to me. Like I'm not good enough. (*Pause.*) I can't afford to come, Luke, and I don't wanna leave me dad.

Pause.

LUKE. You should've just said.

CHRISTIE. I did.

LUKE. I can . . . me Da'd lend you the –

CHRISTIE. I'm not comin'.

Long pause.

LUKE. D'yer reckon you will ask her then . . . Julie?

CHRISTIE. I think so, yeah . . . d'yer reckon I should?

LUKE. Defo.

CHRISTIE. D'yer reckon she'd say yeah?

LUKE. Just go for it.

CHRISTIE. You don't reckon she'd blow me out?

LUKE. I dunno . . . but like, so what even if she does, eh? Just do it, mate.

CHRISTIE. D'yer reckon?

LUKE. Defo. You get blown out, then big fuckin' deal. Get back on your horse, lad. Dennis Michaels. My thirteenth birthday. 1985.

CHRISTIE. He talks fuckin' bollocks, your dad.

LUKE. I know n'all.

Scene Two

June 1989. CHRISTIE*'s bedroom. Small and crammed. The walls are covered in posters. The bed is pushed against the opened window and is slightly smaller than a standard single, with a raised guard at the side that slopes down. There is a wardrobe and a chest of drawers with a record player on the top. LPs are stacked up in piles on the floor.*

CHRISTIE *and* LUKE *are sitting on the bed. They are both wearing suits and swigging from a bottle of red wine. Suddenly,* LUKE *bursts out laughing.*

CHRISTIE. What?

LUKE. Your uncle's fuckin' nuts.

CHRISTIE. Which one?

LUKE. The one with the accordion, yer divvy, who d'yer think? . . . You just lost it in his face, laughing at him. I thought you were cryin'.

CHRISTIE. Jim. He's a tit. Him and me dad hated each other . . . I don't know what him gettin' up and doing a turn was all about. Like he gives a shit. After the church he got hold of me started tryin' to give me all these words of wisdom, like something he says can help. He goes on about 'Death being part of the bargain . . . an' yer have to keep your side.' Fuckin' curtains haven't even stopped swinging. Wanted to chin him.

LUKE. Families are mad like that. Fucking more trouble, mate, than they're worth, better off with . . . sorry, I –

CHRISTIE. Don't worry.

LUKE. I jus' meant.

CHRISTIE. I know, it's sound. Yer right anyway.

Silence.

LUKE. Eh, least you've got a suit now . . . you could take Julie Bridges out somewhere proper.

CHRISTIE. I asked her.

LUKE. Dark horse. When?

CHRISTIE. Couple of weeks ago.

LUKE. What'd she say?

CHRISTIE. What d'yer think?

LUKE. No?

CHRISTIE. Yeah. No.

LUKE. Shit. How come?

CHRISTIE. She doesn't fancy me.

LUKE. Is that what she said?

CHRISTIE. No but she doesn't. She said she's got loads of work.

LUKE. Here y'are then . . . loads of work. Girls are like that about homework. 'Specially girls like Julie Bridges. Fuckin' homework-mad.

CHRISTIE. Come off it. There's only one reason why someone doesn't wanna go out with someone else, Luke. When they don't fancy them.

LUKE. Fridge.

CHRISTIE. I'm not even arsed anyway.

LUKE. Don't be.

CHRISTIE. I'm not.

LUKE. Good.

   Silence.

   Is there no beer? Feel like I'm in church drinkin' red wine . . . S'fuckin rank . . . birds' drink.

CHRISTIE. Downstairs.

LUKE. Will you go?

CHRISTIE. No.

LUKE. Go 'ead, I don't wanna have to talk to anyone.

CHRISTIE. Yeah . . . it must be dead hard for yer, mate . . . oh
hang on, it's my dad that's dead, isn't it?

LUKE. I didn't –

CHRISTIE. It's in the shed, you can go round the side.

LUKE. I'm alright wi' this . . . it isn't that bad after half a
bottle.

Silence.

Eh, d'yer remember Jamie Thomas. From primary school?

CHRISTIE. Yeah.

LUKE. D'yer remember when he got the back of his ankle
bitten off by a monkey in Chester Zoo?

CHRISTIE. Fuckin' 'ell, yeah.

Pause.

LUKE. Were you a bit jealous?

CHRISTIE. No.

LUKE. I was.

CHRISTIE. How come?

LUKE. When he came back and that. When his bandage came
off and he used to flash it round. Just thought . . . y'know,
he can still walk fine. He was fuckin' even still good at
footy. You couldn't see it unless he wanted you to. He'd had
this mad thing like, that had happened to him. That
everyone wanted to know about, talk to him about.
Something that made him interestin'.

CHRISTIE. Other things apart from having one ankle make
yer interestin'.

LUKE. Not when you're eight.

Pause.

CHRISTIE. Luke, I'm scared.

LUKE. What of?

CHRISTIE. Not seein' me dad again.

Pause.

What happens, d'yer reckon?

LUKE. I dunno, mate.

CHRISTIE. I don't know what to do.

LUKE *passes him the bottle.*

Where d'yer think he is?

LUKE. I don't know. (*Pause.*) I think they wait until it's like all cooled down in the incinerator thing at the back . . . then they gather the bits . . . ashes like . . . and put it in the thing . . . the urn thing.

CHRISTIE. I meant his soul.

LUKE. Right. Sorry, mate. I don't know.

CHRISTIE. I don't think he's anywhere. That's what makes me scared.

LUKE. Don't be scared.

CHRISTIE. Why not?

LUKE. Just cos . . . It'll be alright.

CHRISTIE. It isn't though. It isn't alright. I don't believe yer can feel people around yer when they're dead. I think they just go and you're left with their face in yer head an' I don't think it's gonna be alright.

LUKE. But it will be. Try not to think about it.

CHRISTIE. I can't not think about it. I do try but I'm lyin' there and if I shut me eyes, the things I'm tryin' not to think about just get clearer and then I open me eyes and it's like when you've been starin' at a bare lightbulb and loads of them dance about in front of yer face. I don't understand . . .

LUKE. Understand what?

CHRISTIE. Anythin'. I don't understand what the fuckin' point of it all is. I just know that I've got forever in me head and

I can't get over it . . . Feel like someone's sat on me chest. Nothin's ever gonna be normal again.

LUKE. It will.

Silence.

Me dad says he'll get me a car next year if I get lessons.

CHRISTIE. Right.

LUKE. It'll be good though, won't it? Havin' wheels . . . up the pullin' power. We can get Julie Bridges with a big fuckin' puddle.

CHRISTIE. Yeah.

LUKE. With girls in the back . . . fit ones, giving her the fuckin' Vs.

CHRISTIE. Yeah.

LUKE. Things'll be better than normal again.

Silence.

I hope I'm not like a spaz when I'm learning. Our Anthony had like seventy lesssons or something like that . . . S'fuckin' stupid that, isn't it? Seventy lessons . . . me dad was going mad, nearly bankrupted him. I reckon I could pull it off in like eight or something. Cos I'm good already, aren't I? Just need a bit of fine tunin' . . . me three-point turn's a bit rusty but I can only practise in our drive . . . that's shit, innit? Get me out on the road, be sound.

CHRISTIE. Yeah.

Pause.

LUKE. Will yer mam be alright?

CHRISTIE. No, she'll be fuckin' terrible.

LUKE. D'yer wanna go down to her?

CHRISTIE. No, she'll be with all them, won't she? Fussin' round. Jeannette and Elaine are staying at ours, fuckin' worse luck.

LUKE. She's fit, your Auntie Elaine.

CHRISTIE. Pack it in.

LUKE. I see her looking at me sometimes. A look . . . you know what I'm on about?

CHRISTIE. She thinks you egged her house at Hallowe'en.

LUKE. Why?

CHRISTIE. Cos you did.

LUKE. Yeah but how does she know?

CHRISTIE. I dunno.

LUKE. You tell her?

CHRISTIE. No.

LUKE. Yer fuckin' better hadn't 'ave.

Silence.

We're gonna 'ave a good one, yer know.

CHRISTIE. Good what?

LUKE. Summer. It's gonna be good. You an' me. A new start.

CHRISTIE. Feels like the end.

LUKE. Well, it isn't, mate . . . It's the fuckin' beginning.

CHRISTIE. Of what?

LUKE. Life. No more feelin' like a div at school.

CHRISTIE. Thought yer wanted to stay on . . . feel like a div in sixth form.

LUKE. I'm not fuckin' goin' back, doin' more resits. What for?

CHRISTIE. Yer might not have to go back. Yer might have passed.

LUKE. I haven't passed.

CHRISTIE. How yer so sure?

LUKE. I didn't write owt.

CHRISTIE. Nothin' ?

LUKE. Me name. Over and over. In little columns.

CHRISTIE. In all of them?

LUKE. All apart from Science.

CHRISTIE. That's one then –

LUKE. In that one I wrote 'Science is fucking pointless.' Over and over. In little columns.

CHRISTIE. How can yer say Science is pointless, Luke?

LUKE. Name me one job, right, where yer've gotta know how to use a Bunsen burner?

CHRISTIE. Are you just tryin' to wind me up?

LUKE *starts laughing.*

LUKE. Didn't know any of the answers.

CHRISTIE. Yes yer did.

LUKE. Couldn't see the point.

CHRISTIE. There's a fuckin' massive point.

LUKE. If yer you.

CHRISTIE. Yer fuckin' stupid.

LUKE. That's why I didn't write owt –

CHRISTIE. For not putting the answers in . . . you could've walked them. Yer soft bastard.

LUKE. Yeah, whatever.

CHRISTIE. I'm not getting at yer, I'm just –

LUKE. I know.

Silence.

Dennis is on at me about joining up.

CHRISTIE. Joining up what?

LUKE. Me handwriting . . . what d'yer fuckin' think?

CHRISTIE. I dunno, do I?

LUKE. The army.

CHRISTIE. Get lost.

LUKE. Went down the jobby wi' him the other day an' they had a stall.

CHRISTIE. A stall?

LUKE. Yer know, like givin' leaflets out an' that. Recruitin'. Good for the soul, Dennis reckons. Gives yer structure. Character-building. Fuck that.

CHRISTIE. An' did yer tell him fuck that?

LUKE. Course I did. When I get me car we could drive abroad. I could get a convertible. No problems.

CHRISTIE. Aren't yer too young anyway?

LUKE. Getting driving lessons for me seventeenth.

CHRISTIE. For the army.

LUKE. No. I'm not goin', so it isn't even a fuckin' issue anyway.

CHRISTIE. Better hadn't be.

CHRISTIE *stands up swaying, a bit too pissed, before steadying himself and bending down under the bed. He pulls out a shoebox and tips the contents; mostly photos and scraps of paper onto the floor. He rummages through the photos, picks one out and hands it to* LUKE.

LUKE. How old is he there?

CHRISTIE. My age.

LUKE. He's the spit, in' he? Could be you.

CHRISTIE *takes the photo back off* LUKE *and puts everything back into the box before shoving it back under the bed. He lies face down on the floor, his arms stretched out.*

What yer doin'?

CHRISTIE. I'm gonna get an album . . . keep 'em all safe. Do it chronologically from me dad when he was young to growing up to having me. Like a circle. Him at the beginning, me at the end.

LUKE. D'yer feel sick or somethin'?

CHRISTIE. S'comfy. (*Beat.*) Me mum'll live on her own if I leave home.

LUKE. She'll be OK, yer know.

CHRISTIE. She'll put Christmas decorations up on her own.

LUKE. She's got people. You, yer aunties . . . people round her.

CHRISTIE. She'll sleep on her own.

LUKE. She'll be OK.

CHRISTIE. I feel pissed.

LUKE. Pissed good or pissed . . . horrible.

CHRISTIE. Pissed. I had whiskey before. Doesn't agree with me, whiskey. I've nicked a bottle. Stashed it in the wardrobe for us.

LUKE. Sound.

CHRISTIE. Get fucked.

LUKE. No problems.

CHRISTIE. Crate of snowballs there too.

LUKE. Puff.

CHRISTIE. You necked five of them last time you were in ours.

LUKE. Cos there was fuckin' nothin' else.

CHRISTIE. Whiskey now, if you want.

LUKE. Sound.

CHRISTIE. Get fucked.

Pause.

LUKE. I'm sorry, mate . . . about yer dad. It's fuckin' well shit. I'm not . . . I know I'm not all that good at being like . . . saying the right things. I know that . . . but I think about it . . . all the time, mate, I do. Swear. Think about what it's like and I don't know and I'm lucky cos of that. Cos I don't know . . . I don't know.

CHRISTIE *curls up and starts to cry,* LUKE *gets off the bed and kneels down.*

Here y'are, mate . . . don't be . . . c'mon, it's alright. (*He puts his arms awkwardly around* CHRISTIE. *He holds him.*) We'll be fucking sorted . . . you and me. No problems. Things will be normal again.

Scene Three

July 1989. CHRISTIE's *bedroom. Two figures;* CHRISTIE *and* JULIE *are lying next to each other. Motionless. Silence for a few seconds before* CHRISTIE *starts to shift about.*

CHRISTIE. Sorry.

JULIE. What for?

CHRISTIE. Movin' . . . fidgetin' about.

JULIE. Don't be. You're dead still. I've slept with some right fidgeters.

Pause.

Girls. Mates an' that . . . me sister.

CHRISTIE. What?

JULIE. When I said that then . . . about sleeping with people who . . . fidgeters an' that . . . I meant, like me sister and me mates. Girls. Sleeping with girls, mates an' that . . . I didn't mean . . . men . . . boys or anything . . . I haven't –

CHRISTIE. Oh right. I didn't even think nothin'.

JULIE. I know . . . I just thought, God . . . sounds a bit . . .

CHRISTIE. Nah.

Silence.

It's not even a single bed this, yer know.

JULIE. Eh?

CHRISTIE. This isn't even a single bed.

JULIE. How d'yer mean?

CHRISTIE. It's littler.

JULIE. It's littler than a single bed?

CHRISTIE. Yeah. Not shorter . . . just narrower. It's two foot six.

JULIE. Have you had it since you were dead small?

CHRISTIE. Yeah. 'Bout six or somethin'.

JULIE. Aaah. It's got a Banana Splits sticker on this side.

CHRISTIE. Has it?

JULIE. I used to love the Banana Splits.

CHRISTIE. Yeah. They're alright . . . can't remember really. Just remember the song they did.

JULIE. Oh yeah . . . what did it go like?

CHRISTIE. I can't remember the words –

JULIE. The bit in the middle though, what was that? It didn't have words, it was where they –

CHRISTIE. The 'nah nah' bit?

JULIE. Yeah, that's it. What did that go like?

Pause.

CHRISTIE. 'Nah nah nah, nah na na nah, nah nah nah na na na na nah.'

Silence.

JULIE. That was it, yeah.

Silence.

CHRISTIE. Are you alright?

JULIE. Fine.

A barely audible noise from CHRISTIE.

Pardon.

CHRISTIE. Nothing.

JULIE. Did yer wanna say –

CHRISTIE. No. It wa' just a cough.

He moves his arm round her ever so slowly.

Is that –

JULIE. Fine.

Pause.

CHRISTIE. I got in college. Art and English.

JULIE. How come yer didn't say before?

CHRISTIE. I dunno . . . I forgot, I think.

JULIE. How d'yer forget that, Christie?

CHRISTIE. I wasn't . . . I just knew I would.

JULIE. Big-'ead.

CHRISTIE. No . . . I'm not being – I just knew I would.

JULIE. Cos yer brilliant.

CHRISTIE. No I'm not. I'm gonna do just them two, then do Art Foundation.

JULIE. Literature or language?

CHRISTIE. Language. Write some of me own things.

JULIE. Will yer write something for me?

CHRISTIE. What like?

JULIE. Anything. Stories, letters . . . poems.

CHRISTIE. Yeah. If yer want me to . . . if yer won't laugh.

JULIE. Course I won't.

CHRISTIE. Might write yer a song.

JULIE. Will yer sing it to me?

CHRISTIE. Might, yeah.

JULIE. Didn't know yer could write songs.

CHRISTIE. Me dad were in a band.

JULIE. Was he?

CHRISTIE. In the sixties.

JULIE. What were they called?

CHRISTIE. Rockin' Robin and the Redbreasts.

JULIE. Was yer dad Robin?

CHRISTIE. No, there wasn't a Robin. They were rubbish anyway. Me dad was dead good but they were shite.

Pause.

JULIE. I like it . . . here. I like being here.

CHRISTIE. I like yer being here.

JULIE. S'like hidin' away. I could do it for days, make a little nest.

A loud series of bangs as stones are thrown at the window. CHRISTIE jumps up and dashes over to the window, opening it and shouting out into the street.

CHRISTIE. What you doing, dickhead?

LUKE (*offstage*). Yer mum still at yer auntie's?

CHRISTIE. Yeah but the fuckin' neighbours aren't.

LUKE. Let's in.

CHRISTIE. What for?

LUKE. Just let's in.

CHRISTIE. What's up?

LUKE. Come down.

CHRISTIE. What you doin'?

LUKE. Fuckin' . . . open the door.

CHRISTIE. Hold on.

Stumbling, CHRISTIE *pulls on tracksuit bottoms and heads out of the room.*

JULIE. What's going on?

CHRISTIE. Nothin' . . . sorry, it's just Luke –

JULIE. He's not comin' in, is he?

CHRISTIE. Just downstairs . . . just seeing what he wants. He won't come up.

JULIE. Don't let him come up.

CHRISTIE. I won't.

JULIE. I don't want him coming up. Seeing me.

CHRISTIE. He won't. I'll tell him.

JULIE. What if he wants the loo?

CHRISTIE. He'll go the bathroom.

LUKE (*offstage, shouting*). Chris . . . come on, man.

CHRISTIE. Bollocks, he'll wake the street. (*Out of the window.*) You'll wake the fuckin' street. He won't come up.

JULIE. Don't let him.

CHRISTIE. I won't.

JULIE. Don't. Please.

CHRISTIE *exits and runs downstairs. The door can be heard opening. As footsteps are heard thudding up the stairs,* JULIE *dives under the covers, trying to hide herself as much as possible.* LUKE *enters first, drunk, and throws himself onto the bed, breathless.* JULIE *screams.*

LUKE. Fuckin' 'ell.

CHRISTIE *enters.* LUKE *stands, revealing* JULIE *wearing a T-shirt pulled over her knees, curled up in a ball.*

CHRISTIE. What you doing?

LUKE. Alright, love. (*To* CHRISTIE.) Nice one, mate.

CHRISTIE. Shurrup, Luke.

LUKE. Dark horse.

CHRISTIE. What yer doin'?

LUKE. Sayin' 'ello. Thought she didn't fancy yer?

CHRISTIE. Come downstairs?

LUKE. Sorry, Janet. I come to see Christie a minute . . . sorry to interrupt. If I'd known . . . yer never said. He never said. He tells me everything. Usually.

JULIE. It's Julie.

LUKE. Sorry, Julie.

CHRISTIE. Luke.

LUKE. I'll get off in a minute.

CHRISTIE. Yeah, yer will. (*To* JULIE.) He'll get off in a minute.

LUKE (*pulls two cans from each of his pockets*). Want one?

CHRISTIE. No.

LUKE. Julie?

JULIE. No. Thanks.

CHRISTIE. Will you fuck off, Luke. Yer can't just barge –

LUKE. I didn't know there was anything to barge in on, did I? Sorry, Julie.

JULIE. I feel a bit . . . sick.

CHRISTIE. Do you want some water?

JULIE. No, I might just –

LUKE. How's Shelley?

JULIE. She's alright.

LUKE. Nice one. Reckon she'd come on a double date. Four of us. Be a laugh that.

JULIE. I don't know. I want . . . I need to go the bathroom. Could yer just . . . could yer . . . shut yer eyes. Please.

CHRISTIE. Luke.

LUKE. Go on, I'm not lookin'.

JULIE *scrambles across the bed and out of the door, tugging to pull the T-shirt as far down as possible. She slams the door.*

Crackin' pair of legs, mate. Fuckin' 'ell, I can't believe –

CHRISTIE. What the fuck are you playing at, eh?

LUKE. I didn't know . . . if you didn't tell me then how the hell am I meant to know, eh? You do my 'ead in at times.

CHRISTIE. You can't stay.

LUKE. How come?

CHRISTIE. Cos yer can't.

LUKE. There's no one in.

CHRISTIE. Me and Julie are in.

LUKE. Fuckin' get you. 'Me and Julie.' You only fucked her five minutes ago.

CHRISTIE. Shush yer fuckin' mouth, will yer?

LUKE. She can't hear you, mate. She's in the bog.

CHRISTIE. Give us a break, will yer.

LUKE. Give us a fuckin' break then. Fuckin' yer best mate off for a bird.

CHRISTIE. Shurrup. We never anyway.

LUKE. Never what?

CHRISTIE. Had sex. And I saw yer on Tuesday, don't be putting mad guilt trips on me, Luke.

LUKE. I'm not . . . I'm not. Sorry.

Pause.

CHRISTIE. S'fuckin' on top.

LUKE. Sorry, mate.

CHRISTIE. S'OK.

Pause.

Yer alright like?

LUKE. Yeah.

CHRISTIE. Yer just pissed?

LUKE. Bit, yeah . . . not much.

CHRISTIE. Can yer just –

LUKE. Down in one, mate.

LUKE *lies back on the bed.*

CHRISTIE. Luke.

LUKE. Yeah. Fair enough. Point taken.

CHRISTIE. I'll knock round tomorrow.

LUKE. I won't be at home.

CHRISTIE. Where'll yer be?

LUKE. Dunno.

CHRISTIE. What's goin' on?

LUKE. Nothin'. Left for a bit, s'all. Doin' me fuckin' 'ead in.

LUKE *stands.* CHRISTIE *notices a small cut on his forehead.*

CHRISTIE. What happened to yer 'ead?

LUKE. Nothin' . . . borin' usual . . . Had a big fuckin' scrap wi' Dennis.

CHRISTIE. 'Bout what?

LUKE. Nothin' . . . everythin' . . . stuff.

CHRISTIE. Like what?

LUKE. Like . . . wha' I'm doin' wi' me life. Gonna end up on the dole like our Anthony cos I'm a thick cunt, all that shite. Told 'im I've been thinkin' 'bout college . . . doin' resits then somethin' proper afterwards like but he just starts goin' on about doin' somethin' proper now. (*Beat.*) Kept sayin' 'adult' loads like yer do to kids . . . Borin' me to death . . . Anyway told him to fuckin' shut it in the end. Clipped me. Cunt.

Silence.

Wanted to smack him back so I wen' out.

CHRISTIE. Yer alright like?

LUKE. Yeah . . . big pussy, in'he?

CHRISTIE. What yer gonna do now then?

LUKE *shrugs.*

LUKE. Knock somewhere else.

CHRISTIE. Where's that?

LUKE. A mate's.

CHRISTIE. Yer haven't got any.

LUKE. Cheeky cunt.

CHRISTIE. That yer can just knock up at half four in the morning, I meant. Apart from me.

LUKE. Wouldn't 'ave said you 'ad a bird 'til I come in here and sat on her.

CHRISTIE. Yer can get on the couch.

LUKE. Thought yer mam was at Jeanette's?

CHRISTIE. She is.

LUKE. Can't I get in her bed then?

CHRISTIE. No. She'll know. She said it stunk of Brut last time. An' she's back first thing.

JULIE has appeared in the bedroom doorway, wearing a flowery dressing gown.

JULIE. I borrowed this from back of yer mum's door.

CHRISTIE. S'OK.

LUKE. S'nice, that.

LUKE gets a look from CHRISTIE.

What?

JULIE. I might go home now.

CHRISTIE. No, don't . . . he's going downstairs.

JULIE. I know but –

LUKE. I'm goin' downstairs now, Janet, honest . . . just finishing this.

CHRISTIE. Get back into bed.

JULIE. I'll sit on the floor for now.

CHRISTIE. No, don't. Here y'are. I'll sit on the floor 'til he's finished that. You get in.

JULIE. No I'm –

CHRISTIE. No go on, please.

He stands up and after a couple of seconds' hesitation, JULIE clambers into the bed still wearing the dressing gown. CHRISTIE sits on the floor with LUKE.

LUKE (*passing the other can to CHRISTIE*). Go 'ead, yer might as well, I'll take it down wi' me if yer don't want it all.

CHRISTIE. Julie, d'yer –

JULIE. No thanks.

CHRISTIE. Just a swig then down, yeah? You nearly finished that?

LUKE. Easy mate, twenty-five per cent extra free, I'm not a fuckin' fish. Yer can drown drinkin' quick, yer know.

CHRISTIE. No yer can't.

LUKE. Yer can . . . or in a puddle. Something fucking stupid anyway. Like yer'd have to be a right fuckin' feeble 'ead . . . like Barry Morgan or someone. Proper wet lettuce.

JULIE. He's my cousin.

Luke. Is he? Fuckin' 'ell. (Beat.) Sound. What's he up to?

JULIE. He's going to catering college.

LUKE *tries not to laugh but fails.*

What's wrong with that?

LUKE. Nothin'.

CHRISTIE. Just ignore him.

LUKE. Sorry. I'm just in one of them moods. Y'know, when everythin's funny?

CHRISTIE. No.

LUKE. Me and Christie had one, Julie, the other month when we were at the Clough. Where we go. It's our place like. Where we just go like. A little patch of us.

JULIE. I know. I've been.

LUKE. Where?

JULIE. Boggart's Clough. Christie's took me.

LUKE. Did yer?

CHRISTIE. Yeah. Just showin' where it is.

JULIE. It's nice, I like it. I caught a fish but I put it back.

LUKE. When?

CHRISTIE. Other day. Just went . . . just showin' where it is.

Silence.

JULIE. What happened?

LUKE. How d'yer mean?

JULIE. What happened at the Clough that was funny?

Pause.

LUKE. Doesn't sound funny probably, when yer tell it.

JULIE. Go on. I bet it is.

LUKE. We had mushrooms from the field and this group of people rode past on bikes an' . . . they just looked dead funny like. (*Pause.*) We just got on to like if yer didn't know what a bike was . . . how funny it'd be if yer saw one for the first time.

Silence.

That was it. Told yer it doesn't even sound funny. (*Beat.*) I've finished that now. 'Ave yer got a blanket for the couch?

CHRISTIE. There's some in me mum's chest of drawers. D'yer wanna finish that wi' me?

LUKE. Nah, I'm knackered.

LUKE *stands.*

Night then. Sorry Julie . . . 'bout bargin' in an' that.

JULIE. It's OK.

CHRISTIE. Night. Don't worry about Dennis an' that.

LUKE. Yeah . . . like I would.

LUKE *leaves and shuts the door.*

JULIE. Christie . . . Are yer gettin' back in?

Scene Four

August 1989. Boggart's Clough. CHRISTIE *and* LUKE *sit in just their shorts on little canvas fishing stools outside the tent at the water's edge, they are attaching bait to their fishing rods.* CHRISTIE *is struggling and* LUKE *takes over.*

LUKE. Here y'are.

He holds the rod out, CHRISTIE *is staring ahead.*

Take it.

CHRISTIE *takes the rod in his hand, casting it into the water,* LUKE *follows.*

CHRISTIE. And then sometimes it's as if it hasn't even happened or not even that . . . like something really fuckin' ace has happened, like she's dead happy. But I know it's OK. I know that's just what happens now and she's not going mad or anythin'.

LUKE. You alright though?

CHRISTIE. Yeah . . . m'alright.

LUKE. Cos you can like . . . talk y'know . . . to me. I mean, I know yer do but usually it's stuff about yer mum an' that. Yer can talk about . . . you.

CHRISTIE. I know. Ta. (*Pause.*) Julie's quite good with stuff like that.

LUKE. Is she?

CHRISTIE. Yeah.

LUKE. An' d'yer talk to her like?

CHRISTIE. Yeah. Sometimes. Not . . . loads like.

Pause.

LUKE. Sound.

CHRISTIE. Not more than you . . . I haven't felt like talkin' to her more than you. She's just been there when it's come out. I know I can talk to yer.

LUKE. I know.

CHRISTIE. And I do anyway.

Pause.

Don't I?

LUKE. Yeah.

Pause.

Not as much lately. Yer haven't said –

CHRISTIE. Feel a bit better lately, s'all. Just feel –

LUKE. Good.

Pause.

CHRISTIE. Are you hungry?

LUKE. Stupid question.

CHRISTIE. What've yer got?

LUKE. Have a look.

CHRISTIE. Classics?

LUKE. Have a look.

CHRISTIE. What did yer take?

LUKE. Just emptied the tin out. Fuckin' 'ave a look.

CHRISTIE *crawls inside the tent. He rustles around for a minute before emerging with two packets of biscuits.*

CHRISTIE. Rich tea.

LUKE. You bring 'em from now on then.

CHRISTIE. Don't do biscuits in our house. Don't do anything in our house. They're alright anyway . . . Rich tea. I wasn't saying it in a bad way.

LUKE. She doesn't really like me that much, does she?

CHRISTIE. Who?

LUKE. Julie.

CHRISTIE. Yeah. She does, yeah.

LUKE. No she doesn't.

CHRISTIE. She does.

LUKE. S'alright. I'm not offended. Don't blame her anyway. (*Beat.*) You keep us apart. Like you're havin' an affair.

CHRISTIE. No I don't . . . Para. You talk bollocks, you do.

LUKE. Who's the mistress and who's the wife?

CHRISTIE. You're weird.

LUKE. Well, I've gotta be the wife cos I've been around longer.

CHRISTIE. Shut up.

LUKE. Have a laugh.

CHRISTIE. I'm fuckin' . . .

LUKE. What?

CHRISTIE. I have a laugh. Yer just . . . wind me up sometimes.

Pause.

She does like yer anyway.

LUKE. Right.

Pause.

How come?

CHRISTIE. What d'yer mean, how come?

LUKE. What's she said?

CHRISTIE. She likes yer. Thinks yer sound.

LUKE. Even after the other week . . . comin' in the bedroom an' that?

CHRISTIE. Yeah.

LUKE. She doesn't.

CHRISTIE. Like yer?

LUKE. Yeah. She'll tell you she does but she doesn't. It'll all come out soon . . . give it a few more months.

CHRISTIE. She wouldn't lie.

LUKE. She's not Mother fuckin' Teresa, Chris.

CHRISTIE. She fuckin' thinks yer alright. Can we drop it now? Fuckin' hell. Why d'yer care anyway?

Silence. CHRISTIE *takes his fishing rod out of the water. He rolls himself a spliff.*

LUKE. Saw that bloke.

CHRISTIE. Who?

LUKE. Bloke. Army knobhead.

CHRISTIE. What for?

LUKE *shrugs.*

What happened?

LUKE. Nothin'.

CHRISTIE. What'd he say?

LUKE. Just talked to me about it all.

CHRISTIE. Sayin' what?

LUKE. Yer know . . . its a 'proper career' . . . travellin' all over the place an' all that. Just talkin' about it . . . I'd be Private Soldier . . . After trainin' like.

Silence.

Private Soldier Michaels. (*Beat.*) Sounds quite good that, dunnit?

CHRISTIE. Does it?

LUKE. Not for me though told him. Rather be at home with a spliff than marchin' round some frozen field with a rucksack full o' spuds on yer back.

CHRISTIE. Spuds?

LUKE. That's what they make yer do, yer know? So it's heavy.
I was talkin' to Wilko about it an' he told me. Sergeant
Edwards said –

CHRISTIE. Who the fuck's Sergeant Edwards?

LUKE. The bloke. The one who interviewed me.

CHRISTIE. Thought it was just a chat.

LUKE. It was . . . but they're not gonna call it that, are they?
It's all . . . Yer don't have 'chats' in the army, do yer?

CHRISTIE. Don't yer?

LUKE. Yer know what I mean. Not goin' anyway, am I?

CHRISTIE. But yer had an interview.

LUKE. Goin' through the motions, innit? Show willin', keep
Dennis quiet.

CHRISTIE. What yer gonna do then?

LUKE. Don't know. Wanna get away. Go fruit-pickin' if you'd
come with me.

CHRISTIE. I would, I just don't wanna leave –

LUKE. Don't wanna leave Julie, I know.

CHRISTIE. Me mum. I don't wanna leave me mum.

LUKE. Yeah. Sorry.

CHRISTIE. I'd love to go wi' yer.

LUKE. Next year then?

CHRISTIE. Yeah. Defo.

Pause.

LUKE. I looked in the library about it.

CHRISTIE. What the fuck you doin' in the library?

LUKE. I wanted to find out about it, they've got books –

CHRISTIE. Library's do tend to, yeah –

LUKE. About where yer can go . . . what yer can do and how yer . . . there's this place in France, right, where yer stay in the barn or whatever it is . . . it's got beds an' that, yer know, yer don't have to sleep on bales of hay or nothin' . . . but it's in this field and yer sleep there and then get up about five . . . six o'clock in the mornin' and work until about two and then do what yer like. Yer don't really get paid but yer get put up an' fed an' yer don't need anythin', do yer? Middle of nowhere. Just up and out and straight into it. I like the idea of getting up that early.

CHRISTIE *laughs*.

I do. When there's somethin' worth gettin' up for . . . whenever we stay here I always stick me head out the tent, have a little potter round. Watch the sun comin' up. It's like when it's that early, the day seems like one massive . . . I don't know. Like no one's in on it apart from you. Fuckin' . . . freedom or somethin'. I'd love that. (*Pause.*) What? Do I sound like a wanker or something?

CHRISTIE. No. Sounds brilliant.

LUKE. Yeah . . . probably be shite though, won't it? Yer always imagine somethin' different in yer head, don't yer? S'like I'm gettin' it on with the farmer's daughter an' everythin' and she's got hot pants and a fuckin' . . . checked what-d'yer-call-it? Gingham top on, an' plaits and we go swimmin' in the river every day wi' nothin' on and get pissed in the sun. It makes me feel . . . I just wanna live like that, I reckon. For a bit. Before yer've got to start doin' it fer real. (*Beat.*) What's that stuff yer dad used to give us to drink?

CHRISTIE. Kir.

LUKE. Kir, yeah . . . She's not gonna be there though, is she?

CHRISTIE. Dunno unless yer go, do yer?

LUKE. Suppose so. Might have a sister for you n'all.

CHRISTIE. She might, yeah.

LUKE. Or not. Wouldn't care anyway. We'd have a right buzz by ourselves. (*Pause.*) W'unt we?

CHRISTIE. Yeah.

LUKE. Just bein' outside.

Silence. CHRISTIE *picks up the fishing rod and starts to pack it away.*

What yer doin'?

CHRISTIE. It's quarter to five.

LUKE. So?

CHRISTIE. Goin' to Julie's for tea, meetin' her mam an' all that.

Silence.

LUKE. You could do yer paintin'.

CHRISTIE. Eh?

LUKE. France.

Pause.

CHRISTIE. Could, yeah.

LUKE. We could take the tent.

CHRISTIE. Yeah.

LUKE. Get pissed on . . . what's-it –

CHRISTIE. Kir.

LUKE. Get pissed on Kir.

Pause.

CHRISTIE. Yeah.

Scene Five

September 1989. Late afternoon. Boggart's Clough. LUKE is sitting on his own. Waiting. After a bit, JULIE approaches behind him. He knows she is there but doesn't acknowledge her. She sits down beside him and he nods at her. They're silent for a while.

JULIE. I like it here.

Pause.

D'you? I mean, you must like it because –

LUKE. S'alright, yeah.

JULIE. It used to give me the creeps a bit, dunno why but –

LUKE. S'the Boggart.

JULIE. What d'yer mean?

LUKE. Boggart's Clough. Like a little . . . sprite, goblin thing. It's his, the Clough. He like . . . owns it. If he doesn't like yer, he lets yer know. Makes things a bit . . .

JULIE. Where d'yer hear that?

LUKE. Just how it is.

JULIE. Yer don't believe it though, really.

LUKE shrugs.

Well, I don't feel like that any more. He must have decided he likes me or somethin', eh?

LUKE. Maybe yeah.

Pause.

JULIE. How long 'ave yer been comin'?

LUKE shrugs.

Christie reckons it's years an' years. Since you were old enough to go out on yer own.

LUKE. What yer askin' for then?

Pause.

JULIE. He exaggerates sometimes . . . I was just wondering if it was . . . that long like.

LUKE. Probably, yeah . . . if he says. He's got a better memory than me.

Pause.

JULIE. Should I go the phone box?

LUKE. Why?

JULIE. Ring his house.

LUKE. What for?

JULIE. He's late.

LUKE. He's always late.

JULIE. He hasn't been. Not for me. Not so far.

LUKE. It'll wear off.

JULIE. I hope not.

LUKE. Doesn't mean owt . . . Like he's fed up wi' yer or anythin'. Just the way he is. Always has been.

Silence.

Know what that's called?

JULIE. Which?

LUKE. That one there . . . looks a bit like Johnny Rotten.

JULIE. Yeah. (*Beat.*) No, I don't.

LUKE. It's a grebe.

JULIE. A grebe?

LUKE. Yep.

JULIE. It's funny-looking, isn't it?

LUKE. I love the way they sort of dance about on top of the water, bit like they're havin' a fuckin' eppy or summat. They're mad, grebes. If I was a bird, I'd be a grebe.

JULIE. I've never seen one before, I don't think.

LUKE. Have now.

JULIE. Yeah.

Pause.

What's that one?

LUKE. What one?

JULIE. That little tiny one there with the red bit on his head.

LUKE. A goldcrest. (*Beat.*) Smallest bird in Britain.

JULIE. Is it?

LUKE. Yeah.

JULIE. How come yer know so much about birds?

LUKE. Just like wildlife. I used to want to be a zookeeper but
then I realised that's got nothing to do with wildlife. That's
just animals in cages. I wanna see them where they're
supposed to be. I know loads o' things about animals . . . all
different kinds. Only thing that really sticks in me head.

JULIE. Yer could be a . . . marine biologist . . . or somethin'.

LUKE. Did yer know that camels cry real tears?

JULIE. Aah, no. (*Beat.*) What do they cry about?

LUKE. Mostly it's when one of their mates dies. They just
lose it.

JULIE. My grandad's dog pined to death after me grandad
died. Wouldn't eat.

LUKE. Did it cry though?

JULIE. She whimpered loads but there weren't like . . . tears.

LUKE. Camels get proper tears.

JULIE. Aah.

LUKE. I know . . . dead tight, innit?

Pause.

What d'you wanna be?

Pause.

JULIE. I want me own bookshop.

LUKE. What yer gonna call it?

JULIE. Dunno.

LUKE. Gotta have a name for it.

JULIE. I haven't. Can't think of one yet.

LUKE. What sort o' books?

JULIE. Any. All different sorts.

LUKE (*offering a can*). D'yer want some?

JULIE. No. Thanks.

LUKE. D'yer not drink or somethin'?

JULIE. Sometimes. When I'm out somewhere properly.

LUKE. What, yer just pretending now or somethin'?

JULIE. In a pub. At a party. Night-time.

LUKE. Nearly night now.

JULIE. Nearly.

LUKE. S'my favourite time of day, this.

JULIE. Is it?

LUKE. Yeah.

JULIE. How come?

LUKE. Because . . . dunno it just is.

Pause.

The sky goes that colour . . . pinky and a bit smoky and
everything starts to slow down a bit and there's a funny sort
of noise . . . like things settling down. And it smells like . . .
I can't say actually but just like it smells now, d'yer know
what I mean?

JULIE. Yeah, it's nice.

LUKE. And everything's just chilled . . . and the night starts . . . really quietly.

Pause.

JULIE. We've just had our house renovated. And they put a . . . they built an out . . . a conservatory on the back and I thought I was gonna hate it at first, cos it took over the garden and I love our garden but it's got a . . . they put in a glass roof and you can just lie there and look up at the sky.

LUKE. Like now 'cept there's no glass in the way.

JULIE. Yeah. (*Beat.*) But it's a bit warmer and you can lie on the couch . . . and it's not damp.

LUKE. Thought yer liked it here.

JULIE. I do. I'm just sayin' about the conservatory. (*Beat.*) I like it here a lot.

Pause.

LUKE. D'yer want me jacket?

JULIE. No I'm alright, ta.

LUKE *takes his jacket off and hands it to* JULIE. *He's got another thinner jacket on underneath.*

LUKE. Here y'are. Got two on.

JULIE. Thanks.

LUKE. S'Berghaus.

JULIE. Right.

LUKE. Waterproof. You can lie back now. Be as good as the conservatory.

JULIE *tentatively lies back. A couple of seconds later so does* LUKE, *a few feet away.*

Warm?

JULIE. Yeah. Ta.

Silence.

D'y'ever get that feelin' yer gonna fall off? (*Pause.*) D'yer know what I mean . . . when you lie on the ground looking up at the sky? S'like yer not in control . . . like yer in space or somethin'. D'yer get those little moments when yer stomach goes?

LUKE. Yeah . . . like yer've gotta hold on or somethin'.

JULIE. Yeah.

LUKE. S'good . . . I like it.

JULIE. Yeah.

LUKE. Gotta keep lookin' straight up at the sky, though. (*Beat.*) Looks like it's dead near, though, doesn't it? Like yer could touch it. Grab hold of a cloud.

Silence.

JULIE. Luke . . . can I ask yer somethin'?

LUKE. What?

JULIE. Are yer . . . frightened?

Pause.

LUKE. What of?

JULIE. Goin' away.

Long pause.

LUKE. A bit, yeah. A little bit.

They lie still, staring upwards.

Scene Six

November 1989. CHRISTIE*'s bedroom.* JULIE *and*
CHRISTIE *are in bed side by side, a little awkwardly. There is
a few moments silence before they begin to speak.*

JULIE. I don't really feel any different.

CHRISTIE. Are yer meant to, though? Isn't that just what
people say . . . like in magazines and stuff.

JULIE. It didn't hurt, I mean. It's meant to kill, isn't it?

CHRISTIE. I dunno.

JULIE. S'what they say.

CHRISTIE. Is it? (*Beat.*) That's good then, isn't it?

JULIE. Yeah.

   Silence.

   I don't feel older.

CHRISTIE. Yer not.

JULIE. I am. Every second. (*Beat.*) Were yer a bit scared? Not
  – just a little bit like . . . nervous?

CHRISTIE. No.

JULIE. Means yes.

CHRISTIE. Means no . . . I wasn't –

JULIE. I'm windin' yer up.

CHRISTIE. Then pack it in.

JULIE. Sorry.

   Pause.

CHRISTIE. S'it . . . alright like?

JULIE. Yeah . . . s'alright. Sort of what I was expectin' really.

CHRISTIE. Right. Sound.

JULIE. Just y'know . . . I think the first time's about getting it over and done with more than anything else, isn't it?

CHRISTIE. Thanks.

JULIE. I'm not being off wi' yer . . . It's nothin' to do wi' you . . . It'll get better.

Silence.

Say something.

CHRISTIE. What like?

JULIE. I don't know.

CHRISTIE. You've thrown me a bit.

JULIE. I didn't mean to . . . I'm just being honest. I think there's too many lies told about you-know-what.

CHRISTIE. Sex?

JULIE. Yeah.

CHRISTIE. Say it then.

JULIE. Say what?

CHRISTIE. Sex. I've never heard yer actually say 'Sex'.

JULIE. Sex. Sex . . . sex sex sex sex sex sex. It sounds funny when you say it over and over, doesn't it? Do yer ever do that with yer name until it scares yer and yer not sure if it really is yer name?

CHRISTIE. No.

JULIE. I do. (*Pause.*) Say something, Christie, I feel funny.

CHRISTIE. I love yer.

JULIE. Do yer?

CHRISTIE. Yeah, course.

JULIE. Yer haven't stopped?

CHRISTIE. Since half an hour ago?

JULIE. People do. All of a sudden. One minute me mum and dad were packing to go to Fuerteventura, havin' a laugh and the next he's confessed to all sorts and they're gettin' divorced.

CHRISTIE. Talk about spoilin' the moment.

JULIE. Sorry.

CHRISTIE. Nothin's changed . . . Can't see how it ever will.

JULIE. Promise?

CHRISTIE. Spit on me life.

JULIE. I don't wanna go home.

CHRISTIE. Stay then.

JULIE. Thought Luke's back.

CHRISTIE. He is. See him in the mornin'. Go the Clough wi' im. Be with his mam tonight.

JULIE. Since when's that stopped yer?

CHRISTIE. He hasn't seen her for ages.

JULIE. Neither have you. Normally on the doorstep before he is.

CHRISTIE. See him in the mornin'.

Pause.

JULIE. Yer won't tell him, will yer?

CHRISTIE. Shurrup.

JULIE. I don't know, do I? Tell him everythin' else.

CHRISTIE. We don't talk about stuff like that.

JULIE. Oh aye, bet yer don't.

CHRISTIE. We don't. Talk about other stuff.

JULIE. Like everything you've got in common?

CHRISTIE. Shurrup, clever dick.

JULIE. I'm joking with yer.

CHRISTIE. It's not funny.

JULIE. It's not funny tryin' to think of things to say for two hours when I'm sat on me own with him makin' pointless conversation.

CHRISTIE. Fuckin' hell. Can we not move on from that night? How long ago –

JULIE. Alright, alright, calm down –

CHRISTIE. I'm meant to just ignore the fact that me mum's havin' a fuckin' . . . cryin' all over the shop, am I? Just shut the fuckin' door on her?

JULIE. I know, I know. Please let's just leave it, eh?

CHRISTIE. I'd love to but you won't stop goin' on about it.

Pause.

JULIE. I mentioned it then and I mentioned it now. That's twice. That's not goin' on about it.

Silence.

CHRISTIE. He likes yer. Probably doesn't show it. That's the way he is. But he does . . . he does like yer.

Pause.

I can tell.

Pause.

JULIE. Not bothered anyway. Not goin' out with 'im, am I? Have yer written me a song yet?

CHRISTIE. Not yet, I'm –

JULIE. I wrote yer a poem.

CHRISTIE. Did yer?

JULIE. Didn't take me too long. Been in me head for ages.

CHRISTIE. Where is it then?

JULIE. Yer can't have it. Not until I get me song.

CHRISTIE. I have to practise it first. I'll practise until it's right and then I'll surprise yer.

JULIE. I'll love it. You're a natural. Got it in the blood, an't yer?

Pause.

You did that mad thing again last night . . . Where you sit up and look around and yer don't know where yer are. It scared me at first . . . it was like you were some zombie or something. Nothing going on behind yer eyes. Just staring. You looked dead sad.

CHRISTIE. I can't remember. I know what yer mean though. I remember it sometimes. Afterwards. S'like a dream. I forget everything. Who I am, where I am, 'bout me dad . . . then I remember bit by little bit but all dead quick over a second or so. Then I wish I hadn't remembered.

JULIE. S'a lot.

CHRISTIE. Just a couple of seconds.

JULIE. S'a lot of stuff, I meant . . . to go through in a couple of seconds. Finding it all out again.

CHRISTIE. Yeah. S'alright though. I feel better when you're 'ere.

JULIE. I put me arms around yer and then you went straight back off. I held on tight.

CHRISTIE. Me mam's back Sunday.

JULIE. S'gone quick, hasn't it?

CHRISTIE. Too quick.

Pause.

JULIE. Can I stay when she's here?

CHRISTIE *shrugs.*

Can yer not ask?

CHRISTIE. S'pose, just . . . feel a bit weird . . . askin'. S'like admittin' to it, innit?

JULIE. Yer don't have to go into detail.

CHRISTIE. We could get the tent out . . . stay at the Clough.

JULIE. I don't wanna stay in a tent, Christie.

Pause.

CHRISTIE. I'll see . . . I'll just –

JULIE. Doesn't matter.

CHRISTIE. We'll live together anyway, won't we? In the end. After college, uni, whatever . . . Get a dead cool flat. I'll be selling loads of paintings and I'll be in a band.

JULIE. Will yer?

CHRISTIE. Yeah.

JULIE. What'll I be doin'?

CHRISTIE. Yer can come an' watch me, can't yer?

JULIE. For meself. What job will I have?

CHRISTIE. Whatever yer want to do.

JULIE. I know . . . but what do I wanna do, Christie?

CHRISTIE. S'up to you, isn't it? I dunno.

JULIE. Ask me then.

Scene Seven

December 1989. Boggart's Clough. CHRISTIE and LUKE are building a campfire from a stack of wood they have collected. LUKE is wearing a Father Christmas hat. A portable cassette player is on low. They are drinking lager and smoking.

CHRISTIE. What happens?

LUKE. Just takin' it all in, yer know. Learnin' how to –

CHRISTIE. Shoot people?

LUKE. How to be a soldier.

CHRISTIE. Private Soldier Michaels.

LUKE. Yeah.

CHRISTIE. Right . . . then what?

LUKE. Dunno. Do it, I s'pose.

CHRISTIE. Do what?

LUKE. Be a fucking soldier, what d'yer think?

CHRISTIE. Could I come and visit yer?

LUKE. What d'yer mean?

CHRISTIE. Come out for a week to Cyprus.

LUKE. Can you fuck? What d'yer think it is, Butlins?

CHRISTIE. D'yer not get time off?

LUKE. I'm in the army, mate. You don't get time off, yer get 'leave'. (*Beat.*) I've got photos.

LUKE *pulls a packet of photographs from his pocket.*

S'a Saracen.

CHRISTIE. Big.

LUKE. Seventeen foot long. Six an' 'alf foot tall. Just over ten tonne. Goes quick n'all though.

CHRISTIE. Right.

LUKE. Forty-five mile per hour. Yer sit there.

CHRISTIE. Right.

LUKE (*flicks to another photo*). Eight-mill mash there.

CHRISTIE. Yer what?

LUKE. Machine gun. Eight millimetres. The barrel. Like . . . yay big. (*Demonstrates.*)

CHRISTIE. 'Yay big'?

LUKE (*flicks to another photo*). That's an AT105 Saxon. Eleven an' 'alf tonne.

Pause.

CHRISTIE. You been in any of 'em yet.

LUKE. No. (*Flicks to another photo.*) That's Coggo.

CHRISTIE. Right.

LUKE. He's fuckin' hilarious.

CHRISTIE. Why?

LUKE. What d'yer mean, why?

CHRISTIE. Why's he funny?

LUKE. Cos he just is.

CHRISTIE. What's he do?

LUKE. Nothin' . . . he's just, y'know . . . stuff he comes out with.

CHRISTIE. Like what?

LUKE. Fuckin' . . . I dunno . . . things, jokes an' that. He's always playing practical . . . jokes.

CHRISTIE. Like what?

LUKE. Just like . . . stupid shit . . . here y'are, first day he's like, 'Micko – '

CHRISTIE. Micko?

LUKE. ' – you need to go to the admin office to fill in some extra stuff . . . ' – forms and that, that I'd missed apparently. So, I'm well fucked off cos it's a fifteen-minute walk and I've just got me head down . . . but I go off and it's pissing down and I get there . . . fuckin' yer know, piss wet through an' that and you go through the whole thing, regiment name, fuckin' . . . shoe size and they're like, 'No, you've given us all the stuff we need,' an' I said, 'I've been told . . . by this lad, me mate' and the woman's like, 'He's having you on, son.'

CHRISTIE. An' was he?

LUKE. Yeah . . . dickhead.

LUKE *laughs.* CHRISTIE *is silent.*

S'what it's about though, in a way . . . they have this thing
they say . . . 'If you can't take a joke, you shouldn't have
joined' . . . S'what it's about really.

CHRISTIE. A big laugh.

LUKE. Sometimes, yeah.

CHRISTIE. Why didn't you just be a redcoat in Butlins then?

LUKE. I can't sing.

Silence. CHRISTIE *turns 'Fool's Gold' up high on the
cassette player.* LUKE *turns it down.*

We were talkin'.

CHRISTIE. No, we weren't.

LUKE. I was.

CHRISTIE. Go on then.

Silence.

Luke.

LUKE. What?

CHRISTIE. What's the matter?

LUKE. Nothing.

CHRISTIE. Stop being a mardy twat then.

LUKE. I'm not being anythin'.

CHRISTIE. Well, that's even worse. Not being anythin'.

LUKE. Never said I didn't care, did I? I'm just sitting here . . .
not being anythin' in particular. Just sittin'. Is that allowed?

CHRISTIE. Yeah, course.

LUKE (*to painting*). What's that?

CHRISTIE. Crimbo prezzie for Julie. (*Beat.*) It's a paintin'.

LUKE. Can fuckin' see that. D'yer do it yerself?

CHRISTIE. Yeah.

LUKE. What's it meant to be?

CHRISTIE. Nothing really.

LUKE. Is it like . . . how yer feeling?

CHRISTIE. A bit yeah . . . it's like –

LUKE. I feel a bit like that sometimes. (*Short pause.*)
Although I'd lash a bit more purple on it. Little splash o'
yeller on top . . . just a sprinklin'.

CHRISTIE. You takin' the piss?

LUKE. Fuck off. D'yer want me to talk to yer or what?

CHRISTIE. Yeah –

LUKE. Then stop bein' a cunt.

CHRISTIE. You haven't always been into stuff . . . like that . . .
art an' that . . . S'all.

LUKE. Neither've you. Born with a paintbrush in yer hand,
were yer? Fuckin' Picasso.

Silence.

CHRISTIE. You're too much, you, sometimes. Give me
palpitations.

LUKE. S'all about pace. Need to pick yours up a bit, mate.
Stop dragging your heels. Stop smoking gear all fuckin'
day.

CHRISTIE. I do loads of work.

LUKE. That's not work. Paintin's not work, Christie. Paintin's
escaping. You wanna reel yourself back in. Give yerself up.
Only a matter a time before you get caught anyway . . . may
as well fuckin –

CHRISTIE. Wha' you on about, Luke?

Pause.

LUKE. What you gonna do when you leave, eh?

CHRISTIE. Dunno. Somethin'. Somethin' I want.

LUKE. Fat fuckin' chance.

CHRISTIE. Yeah, probably but –

LUKE. Yer don't do what yer want, Christie. S'not the score these days. Yer do what yer told yer can. What's available.

CHRISTIE. Don't –

LUKE. Don't what?

CHRISTIE. You fucking know. It's not fuckin' on, Luke. Just cos –

LUKE. Just cos what? Cos what? Cos what, eh?

CHRISTIE. Calm down, will yer . . . makin' me feel –

LUKE. All I'm sayin' is yer can't just fucking . . . float about. Not making things concrete. Things need to be –

CHRISTIE. Concrete.

LUKE. Yeah.

Pause.

CHRISTIE. What does that mean exactly though? Luke? Concrete.

LUKE. Means . . . Workin' towards somethin' . . . I dunno. Means makin' things . . .

LUKE trails off. He takes his Father Christmas hat off and starts to burn holes in it with his cigarette. CHRISTIE *takes it off him.*

CHRISTIE. Are yer alright, Luke?

LUKE. Yeah.

CHRISTIE. Are yer . . . happy like?

LUKE. Can't remember.

CHRISTIE. What's that mean?

LUKE. What I say . . . (*Pause.*) I mean I can't remember . . . feelin' any different . . . got nowt to compare it to, d'yer get me? I remember things like . . . events an' that when I was a kid but it's like I wasn't actually involved. Like you're watchin' telly or a film or something. Did that once but the other way round . . . get onto this – I was thinking about this big car crash I saw . . . big chase like . . . massive fuck-off collision, red Cortina and a bizzy car . . . proper no-chancer. Proper detail, like feeling excited and shitting meself, standing there in the street fucking gob open. And I thought about it a bit more . . . piecing it together . . . fuckin' episode of *The Sweeney*, wan' it? I wasn't even fuckin' there . . . and it was in black and white.

CHRISTIE. We watched that together.

LUKE. In your front room. With yer dad, yeah?

CHRISTIE. Yeah.

LUKE. Was definitely *The Sweeney*, wan' it?

CHRISTIE. Yeah.

LUKE. I think I felt happy then.

Pause.

CHRISTIE. Can you come home?

LUKE. No.

Scene Eight

July 1990. CHRISTIE's *bedroom.* CHRISTIE *sits on the bed, smoking. He's wearing a T-shirt and baggy shorts and has an old tape recorder on his lap. He fiddles around with it for a while, pressing stop and rewind before speaking into it.*

CHRISTIE. Hiya mate. How yer doin'? Sorry it's been so long . . . I did start a letter but I thought . . . yer can hear me now, can't yer? Hear me voice. (*Beat.*) I done yer a tape of songs but I'll send that seperate, I hope yer into it . . . I think you will be, I put some stuff on 'specially for yer. (*Pause.*) College is good. It's really good actually. We broke up couple o' weeks ago. Get fuckin' ages for summer in college, yer know . . . ten weeks or something mad like that. S'fuckin top. (*Beat.*) In Art, for me last assessment I got a distinction which is like the best yer can get, so that's . . . yer know, good an' that. (*Pause.*) Julie's gone on holiday with her mam, I miss her loads actually an' she's only been gone for like two days . . . S'doin' me head in already. (*He stops, rewinds the tape, starts again.*) Alright mate, how's it goin', yer big fuckin' div? (*He stops, rewinds the tape, starts again.*) Luke, hiya mate . . . S'fuckin' doin me head in, this, keep tryin'a just talk to yer . . . it's dead hard, I wrote a letter but I thought be good, yer know, if yer could hear me voice. What's it like then, eh? Must be . . . (*He stops, rewinds the tape, starts again.*) Alright mate, sorry it's been ages. It doesn't feel like it . . . just goes dead quick, dunnit? Time like. Flies. (*Beat.*) I don't mean that to sound like . . . (*To himself.*) For fuck's sake. (*He stops, rewinds the tape, pauses for a moment, starts again.*) Hi Luke. I do miss yer, yer know. I just want yer to know that I do. I hope yer . . .

Long pause. CHRISTIE *stops the tape, takes it out and chucks it under the bed. He replaces it with a Stone Roses one and presses play. He lies back on the bed.*

Scene Nine

Early December 1990. CHRISTIE*'s bedroom.* JULIE *sits on the bed.* CHRISTIE *enters. He puts his bags down and takes his coat off. His jeans and sweatshirt are splattered with paint. It takes a couple of seconds before he notices her. He jumps.*

JULIE. Sorry.

CHRISTIE. Fuckin' hell . . .

JULIE. What's up?

CHRISTIE. Nothin', just frightened me.

JULIE. It was meant to be a surprise.

CHRISTIE. It was.

JULIE. A nice one.

CHRISTIE. It is.

CHRISTIE *goes over to the bed, kisses* JULIE *and sits down next to her.*

JULIE. Yer mam says you've been out all day.

CHRISTIE. I have.

JULIE. How did yer get on?

CHRISTIE. Fuckin' brilliant.

JULIE. Yeah?

CHRISTIE. Got shit loads done. Wanted to bring it home but it's all still wet. Wanted to show yer. Six little canvases. I felt . . . sound. Capable. S'fuckin good when yer feel good at something, innit?

JULIE. Are yer askin' me or tellin' me?

CHRISTIE. What's up?

JULIE. Nothing.

CHRISTIE. Mardy.

JULIE. I'm not . . . just been waiting ages.

CHRISTIE. I didn't know, did I? Been workin' –

JULIE. It's good. I'm glad it's goin' well. I just wanted to see yer.

CHRISTIE *stands and starts getting changed.*

CHRISTIE. Got covered. Reckon they look quite good like this though.

JULIE. Mine was rubbish.

CHRISTIE. Eh?

JULIE. My day. If yer interested.

CHRISTIE. Course I am. Just gonna ask, wasn't I? If yer give us a chance.

JULIE. Go on then.

CHRISTIE. How was yer day?

JULIE. Me dad's got a girlfriend. I went round. She was putting Christmas decorations up. That's serious, that, isn't it?

CHRISTIE. What's she like?

JULIE. Young.

CHRISTIE. Speak to her?

JULIE. Bit?

CHRISTIE. And?

JULIE. And what?

CHRISTIE. Have yer told yer mam?

JULIE. No.

CHRISTIE. Might be nothin'.

JULIE. He loves her. He told me. I wanted to throw up.

CHRISTIE. Things change.

JULIE. She's called Bernice but he calls her 'Bernie'.

CHRISTIE. It might be OK, yer know . . . it might be –

JULIE. Me mam still blames herself. Thinks he'll come back if she's all smiles when he calls round. He's a fuckin' arsehole.

CHRISTIE. Sorry.

JULIE. S'alright.

CHRISTIE. D'yer wanna go away somewhere?

JULIE. Where?

CHRISTIE. Dunno. Just get on a train or somethin'. Wherever. Somewhere new.

JULIE. OK.

CHRISTIE *sits on the bed, pulls* JULIE *to him and they lie, hugging.*

I can't breathe.

CHRISTIE *lets go. They lie side by side.*

I saw Luke's mum before. She stopped me. I didn't think . . . She said she'd seen me wi' you, out and about. She's nice, isn't she?

CHRISTIE. She's alright, yeah.

JULIE. She was pushin' Anthony's little girl in her pram. She said to say 'ello. She sent her love. Anthony's engaged, yer know?

CHRISTIE. Right.

JULIE. It was Luke's birthday last month. His eighteenth. Did yer . . . I felt a bit funny an' I didn't really know why. (*Pause.*) Christie? Am I talkin' to meself or what?

CHRISTIE. What d'yer want me to say?

JULIE. Why yer bein' like that?

CHRISTIE. I'm tired.

JULIE. You don't even mention him now.

Silence.

CHRISTIE *reaches under the bed and pulls out a packet of photographs, he passes them to* JULIE *then sits on the floor, his back against the bed.*

What are they?

JULIE *opens the packet.*

CHRISTIE. Didn't send a letter. Just them.

JULIE *starts to look through. Long pause.*

JULIE. I feel a bit sick.

CHRISTIE. I did yer a song.

JULIE. Christie.

CHRISTIE. What?

JULIE. Have yer showed anyone?

CHRISTIE. No. You.

JULIE. Have yer spoken to him?

CHRISTIE. Not for a while.

JULIE. What's a while?

CHRISTIE. I dunno.

JULIE. These are –

CHRISTIE. Why d'yer think I haven't shown yer before?

JULIE. I dunno.

CHRISTIE. Cos of this.

JULIE. Cos of what? I'm not saying anything.

Silence.

CHRISTIE. Are yer happy cos yer've proved yer point?

JULIE. I'm not tryin' to prove anythin' –

CHRISTIE. Been right all along.

JULIE. No.

CHRISTIE. Bollocks.

JULIE. I haven't said anything. I think –

CHRISTIE. There's more. All pretty much the same. (*Pause.*) I don't reply.

JULIE. You send tapes.

CHRISTIE. I sent one . . . Months ago. Happy?

JULIE. That doesn't make me happy.

CHRISTIE. I don't care what it makes yer. D'yer want this song or not?

JULIE. I think yer should speak to him . . . write to him or somethin'. I think yer need –

CHRISTIE. I don't need anythin', thanks . . . I don't need tellin' what to do.

JULIE. I'm not telling yer what to do.

Pause.

CHRISTIE. I'm still a bit weird about the words at the moment but I've got a tune sussed. Can play a few chords if yer like.

JULIE. I'm in the middle of talkin'.

CHRISTIE *fetches his guitar which is propped up against the wall and starts to play.*

Chris . . . Christie.

CHRISTIE. Hang on a minute, will yer?

JULIE. I think yer should get in touch or somethin' . . . maybe go and see his mum. I could come with yer if yer wanted.

CHRISTIE *stops playing.*

CHRISTIE. What for? Yer don't even know her.

JULIE. I just think yer need –

CHRISTIE. D'yer want to listen to your song, Julie?

JULIE. No.

CHRISTIE. Can yer just go then, please.

JULIE. What?

CHRISTIE. If yer not gonna listen to yer song, can you leave.

JULIE. I don't want to leave, I want to talk to you about yer friend.

CHRISTIE. If yer not gonna listen to the song I wrote for you, can you get the fuck out of my house? (*Beat.*) Please.

Silence. After a few moments CHRISTIE *starts to play a few chords.* JULIE *stands and leaves, pulling the door behind her.* CHRISTIE *puts the guitar down and lies back on the bed.*

Scene Ten

December 1990. Boggart's Clough. JULIE is sitting huddled, a rucksack next to her feet. It's cold. She is jumping up and down trying to keep warm. LUKE enters.

LUKE. Alright. (*Beat.*) Sorry I'm a bit –

JULIE. Hiya . . . S'OK, only just got here meself really.

LUKE. What yer doin'?

JULIE. Just tryin'a get warm.

LUKE. Fuckin' freezin', innit?

JULIE. Do yer want . . . Shall we go to the pub or somethin'?

LUKE. No . . . I mean, if yer want to like –

JULIE. I don't mind. We might as well just stay here. I've warmed up a bit now.

    LUKE *takes off his scarf and wraps it around* JULIE.

Thanks.

    LUKE *sits and* JULIE *follows.*

I brought some stuff. Butties an' that.

LUKE. Nice one.

JULIE. Coupla cans. D'yer want one? Stella.

LUKE. Go 'ead, yeah.

    JULIE *rummages in the bag and pulls out two cans, opens both and passes one to* LUKE.

This out proper, is it?

JULIE. What? (*Beat.*) Oh aye, yeah . . . it's an occasion, so it's alright.

LUKE. What's that then?

JULIE. Sorry?

LUKE. What's the occasion?

JULIE. Oh, dunno really just . . .

LUKE. I w'ant bein' funny or anythin'.

JULIE. Oh yeah, I know.

Pause.

Thank you. For replying to me letter.

LUKE. S'alright, I didn't expect –

JULIE. I didn't want yer to think I was . . . stickin' me nose in. I wasn't –

LUKE. I didn't, don't . . . think that.

JULIE. Good.

LUKE. I read it lots of times.

JULIE. Did yer?

LUKE. Yeah. I'll keep it.

JULIE. Ta.

LUKE. Mine wasn't . . . you're good at writin' letters. Mine was . . . I didn't know what to put. I mean, I did but it's hard tryin' to –

JULIE. It was a lovely letter.

Pause.

LUKE. Have yer thought what to call it yet?

JULIE. What to call what?

LUKE. Yer bookshop.

JULIE. Don't think I wanna do that any more.

LUKE. How come?

JULIE. I don't know. Had this idea in me head of exactly what it was gonna be like . . . how it smelt and everythin' . . . things are never the same as in yer head, are they?

LUKE. No.

JULIE. I wanna do somethin' else.

LUKE. What?

JULIE. I don't know yet.

LUKE. I thought of a couple o' names.

JULIE. Did yer?

LUKE. Yeah.

JULIE. What are they then?

LUKE. I'm not tellin' yer now you're not doin' it. I'm gonna keep 'em to meself. I might fancy that. I'd make it a specialist one . . . loads of nature books.

JULIE. You'd be good at that.

LUKE. Not gonna happen though.

JULIE. It could do. All yer need to –

LUKE. Is he alright?

JULIE. Yeah . . . he's alright, fine. Busy.

LUKE. I thought . . . part of me. I had this idea he was gonna come with yer and yer weren't telling me.

JULIE. No. Sorry.

LUKE. Like fuckin' Cilla Black *Surprise Surprise*. It's alright.

JULIE. No, it's not . . . I should have –

LUKE. No. Sound. You two alright . . . like together an' everythin'?

JULIE. Yeah.

Pause.

LUKE. He's into college an' that?

JULIE. Yeah. He doesn't know I'm here.

LUKE. No, yeah . . . I didn't reckon.

Pause.

JULIE. I think yer should ring him.

LUKE. Reckon I'll just leave it alone –

JULIE. I think he'd be dead –

LUKE. Julie. Nice one and everythin' but –

JULIE. I saw it. Some of the stuff yer sent. Christie showed me.

LUKE. Wasn't meant for anyone else.

JULIE. He was worried, he wasn't –

LUKE. Well, he should have spoke to me, wrote to me or something, don't wanna be . . . wasn't meant to be for anyone else.

JULIE. Yeah . . . he just got – I think it scared him. I don't think he –

LUKE. Everything fuckin' scares him.

JULIE. They were horrible, them, Luke.

Silence.

Christie thought you sent them cos yer thought they were . . . funny or something, not funny but I think he thought –

LUKE. I did.

JULIE. Think it were funny?

LUKE. Yeah. Yer know the one were Johnsey . . . the lad wi' blond spiky hair, yer know the one where he's bent down and he's pretendin' to light a cigarette stickin' out of that dead bloke's mouth. No arms or legs. That was my idea. For a laugh. I thought that'd be funny.

JULIE. I said that it would've been because –

LUKE. Well, yer shouldn't, should yer? Shouldn't say shit about people when yer don't know them. Who d'yer think yer are anyway? Think you know what goes on in my fuckin' head?

JULIE. No.

Pause.

LUKE. Yer know fuck all, girl.

JULIE. I never said I knew anything. (*Beat.*) What we doin' here, Luke?

LUKE *shrugs. Silence.*

LUKE. That it then, is it? Wi' me and him? (*Pause.*) Got the hump has he? Is he 'disgusted' wi' me?

JULIE. I think he just feels sad.

LUKE. What a fuckin' luxury. (*Pause.*) Could he not tell me that himself like? Fuckin' send the girlfriend down with a fuckin' note. Pussy.

JULIE. He doesn't know I'm here.

LUKE. Fuckin' 'ell . . . that's better, is it? You lie to go and see his best mate and that's meant to make me feel better?

JULIE. Not supposed to make yer feel anything.

LUKE. Fuckin' sat at home listening to Bob Dylan feelin' sad. Fuckin' hell.

Silence.

JULIE. I don't think yer did think it was funny, Luke, taking them photos.

LUKE. Don' t yer?

JULIE. No.

Pause.

LUKE. Did yer say yer brought sarnies wi' yer?

JULIE. Yeah.

LUKE. What are they?

JULIE. Cheese and Branston.

LUKE. Go on then.

JULIE *fetches a sandwich from the bag and passes it to* LUKE.

Ta.

LUKE *eats.* JULIE *stares ahead.*

JULIE. How long –

LUKE. Boxing Day.

JULIE. What are yer going to do?

LUKE. Nothing.

JULIE. Yer can't go –

LUKE. Nothing.

JULIE. Yer need to see somebody who –

LUKE. Nothing. Have yer got any crisps?

JULIE fetches some plain crisps from her bag.

Any flavoured ones?

JULIE. No.

LUKE. Alright. Ta.

He opens the bag and stuffs some in his mouth along with the sandwich. After a few second he puts his head in his hands and starts crying.

Scene Eleven

March 1991. CHRISTIE's bedroom. JULIE is putting bits and bobs into a plastic bag: tapes, a couple of books, the odd item of clothing. CHRISTIE is lying on the bed, staring into space. JULIE holds up a T-shirt, chucks it to CHRISTIE.

CHRISTIE. Yer can 'ave it.

He chucks it back.

JULIE. S'yer favourite.

CHRISTIE. Yer wear it all the time anyway.

JULIE. Cos it's your favourite.

She throws it back at him, he holds onto it.

Where's that box o' tapes?

CHRISTIE. Top drawer.

JULIE opens the top drawer of the chest and gets the box out. She sets it on the floor and starts dividing the tapes into two little piles.

D'yer have to do it like that?

JULIE. Like what?

CHRISTIE. Like that. Two little piles. Yer can have whatever yer like.

JULIE. Just sorting through 'em.

CHRISTIE. Take them all, I'm not bothered.

JULIE. Don't be stupid, Christie.

CHRISTIE. Not arsed.

JULIE. Yes yer are. Only a few are mine anyway.

Pause.

JULIE *starts to put some blank tapes into the cassette player to see what they are. She does this three times before putting in a tape that* CHRISTIE *has made for* LUKE. *It comes on for a few seconds before* CHRISTIE *reaches down and turns it off.*

If yer find me Smiths, will yer post it . . . drop it round or somethin'?

CHRISTIE. Yeah.

JULIE *puts her pile of tapes into a bag, along with the other items she has gathered.*

JULIE. Doesn't look much, does it?

CHRISTIE. No.

JULIE. Thought I had loads here.

JULIE *sits on the bed.*

Can I lie with yer?

CHRISTIE. Yeah.

She lies down next to him. They do not touch.

JULIE. It feels funny, doesn't it?

CHRISTIE. Hilarious.

JULIE. Yer know what I mean.

Silence.

I don't want things to be all weird, Chris . . . I want to – it isn't just me but I feel like I'm the bad one . . . like I'm tryin' to get round yer and it isn't like that . . . it's not what we said. It's both of us . . . and I don't find it easier than you, yer know. I'm just makin' a fuckin' . . . effort.

CHRISTIE. I haven't said anything.

JULIE. Exactly. Just lying there. Are yer not upset or what?

CHRISTIE. Yeah.

JULIE. I can't tell.

Silence.

CHRISTIE. I don't know what to talk about.

JULIE. Forget it.

CHRISTIE. We could go the same uni. You pick. I'm not arsed. Anywhere but here.

JULIE. Don't be daft.

CHRISTIE. I'm not.

JULIE. Yer don't love me.

CHRISTIE. Yes I do.

JULIE. Not in the right way.

CHRISTIE. What's the right fuckin' way?

JULIE. Yer know what I mean. I'm tryin' to be sound here, Chris . . . why d'yer have to be like that? I'm sayin' yer don't have to pretend or anything.

JULIE *stands.*

Where's me jacket?

CHRISTIE. I'm not fuckin' pretendin'.

JULIE. Alright.

JULIE *spots her jacket and puts it on.*

I'm gonna go, Christie.

CHRISTIE. Hang on a minute.

JULIE. There's no point.

CHRISTIE. There is . . . I just –

JULIE. There isn't, Chris. I just wanna –

CHRISTIE. Please.

JULIE. Please what?

CHRISTIE. I want yer to forgive me.

JULIE. What for? What've yer done?

Pause.

CHRISTIE. Everythin's endin'.

JULIE. No it isn't.

Silence. CHRISTIE *stares ahead.*

Chris –

CHRISTIE. I got a letter.

JULIE. From who?

Silence.

CHRISTIE. Off Luke's mum. Few days ago.

JULIE *sits back on the bed. She takes* CHRISTIE's *hand but he pulls away.*

JULIE. What's happened?

CHRISTIE *fetches the letter from the box under his bed. He hands it to* JULIE. *She takes it out of the envelope but doesn't read it.*

Just tell us.

Pause. JULIE *unfolds the paper and reads. When she has finished, she folds the letter carefully and puts it back in the envelope. They sit, side by side, in silence.*

CHRISTIE. He meant it, yer know. He wanted it. It wasn't about –

JULIE. I know –

CHRISTIE. Attention –

JULIE. It's OK. He's comin' back. It'll be –

CHRISTIE. I've had that for days. I've known for days and not done anythin' about it. I've not –

JULIE. He'll be –

CHRISTIE. I have not done anything.

> CHRISTIE *lies face down on the bed and pulls a pillow over his head.* JULIE *sits with her back to him, holding the letter.*

Scene Twelve

October 1991. Boggart's Clough. CHRISTIE *and* LUKE *are sitting side by side. They have been there for some time and are silent for a while before speaking.*

CHRISTIE. You look . . . sound, yer know.

LUKE. Do I?

CHRISTIE. Yeah. Dead good.

LUKE. What did yer expect?

CHRISTIE. I dunno.

> *Pause.*

> Do I?

LUKE. D'yer what?

CHRISTIE. Look –

LUKE. You look like you. So . . . that's good, innit? Wouldn't be good if you looked like someone else.

> *Pause.*

CHRISTIE. How are yer?

LUKE *shrugs*.

Shit?

LUKE. Shit, happy, sad, paranoid . . . bored . . . lots of different stuff.

CHRISTIE. . . .

LUKE. You alright?

CHRISTIE. Fine . . . OK . . . yer know.

LUKE. Not really, no.

Pause.

CHRISTIE. I mean, y'know, not . . . 'Fine' sounds like I'm . . . I'm bein' . . . I wanna talk. There's just a lot to fit in, in't there? I don't know where to start. I'm tryin' but it's hard. Yer can't just launch into it. It's not that I'm . . . I just don't know where the fuck to start. It feels like so long, Luke, I just –

LUKE. Over a year.

CHRISTIE. Is it?

LUKE. Yeah.

Pause. CHRISTIE *fidgets uncomfortably.*

It's alright. No need to be so nervous.

CHRISTIE. I know . . . s'just, it's you. I didn't think . . .

Pause.

LUKE. Didn't think what?

CHRISTIE. I dunno. (*Beat.*) Feel like a mess, man.

LUKE *studies him.*

LUKE. Yer look alright. For an art student.

CHRISTIE. Inside.

LUKE. I did understand. I was lightenin' the mood.

CHRISTIE. Yeah. (*Beat.*) I'm not an art student anyway. Didn't go.

LUKE. What are yer?

CHRISTIE. Nothin' . . . just takin' some time. Thinkin'.

LUKE. That's alright.

CHRISTIE. I know.

LUKE. S'good.

CHRISTIE. I know.

LUKE. Why d'yer look so frightened?

Pause.

CHRISTIE. Cos . . . I am.

LUKE. Why?

CHRISTIE. I dunno. What happens now?

LUKE. With what?

CHRISTIE. Dunno. You. What d'yer –

LUKE. What do I what?

CHRISTIE. D'yer get . . . does anyone . . . help yer?

Pause. LUKE *laughs.*

What?

LUKE. I'm on a list. A waitin' list. To see a 'community psychiatric nurse'. Dunno how long. They give yer some tablets and tell yer to wait. Box ticked. I'm not fuckin' seein' anyone . . . no fuckin' point.

CHRISTIE. It might be good to see someone –

LUKE. Nah.

CHRISTIE. Talk to someone . . . yer need that, y'know.

LUKE. Don't, Christie. Please don't fuckin' tell me what I need. Please don't fuckin' tell me what I need. You've got no idea what –

CHRISTIE. I just meant . . . talkin'.

LUKE. I'm not bein' . . . It's all I've wanted to do really for
ages. Ever. Talk. To yer . . . Since we were kids. Tell yer . . .
but now . . . I don't wanna. An' I especially don't wanna
talk about what's shit, Chris. I don't wanna talk about all
the shit that gives me . . . pains behind me eyes, there aren't
enough . . . words. (*Pause.*) I wanna talk about what's
fuckin' . . . brilliant. (*Beat.*) Bit stumped at this particular
moment like . . . but I know it's there. Somewhere. That's
what I'm hopin'. I'm sort of holdin' onto that. (*Beat.*) Tell
me somethin' normal.

Pause.

CHRISTIE. Me mum went away with me Auntie Elaine. First
time she's been on a proper holiday without me dad and she
loved it. She's doin' sound about him. (*Beat.*) Really sound.
In fact sometimes I –

LUKE. That's good.

CHRISTIE. Yeah. I know. It's good. It's just . . . I had this
dream about him the other month. I was dyin' to tell yer.
(*Beat.*) I thought it was a sign. He proper came to me and
everything. Said even though it was a dream he was really
talking to me and that he'd gone to Brazil for a bit. I could
smell him. And y'know that thing where yer wake up and
for a second it makes total sense and then yer realise . . . it
doesn't.

LUKE. But it sort of does though, doesn't it? Someone told me
this thing, that when yer die . . . when yer go into . . . over
to fuckin' whatever . . . it is. Yer can do whatever yer wanna
do, go anywhere, do these amazing things that life won't let
yer. And then yer think s'got to be that, an' it?

CHRISTIE. Maybe, yeah.

LUKE. Makes more sense than all this fuckin' madness.

Pause.

CHRISTIE. Yer look sound, yer know, Luke, I really –

LUKE. I wanted to . . . Yer asked me about yer dad when he first died and I didn't know what to say. Like I wasn't . . . qualified or somethin'. Never thought about it before . . . apart from me grandad but he was too old and I was too young. Now it's like I fuckin' breathe it and eat it and wrap it around me when I go to bed. Things'll never be normal again.

CHRISTIE. They will, yer know.

LUKE. Nah.

Pause.

When I die, I wanna be an astronaut.

CHRISTIE. Shurrup, Luke.

LUKE. Nothin' stupid again. I mean when I'm old or somethin', get run over . . . accident. Yer just bypass all the training apparently and yer kit's free. And it's not about fucking around with satellites and wreckin' stuff . . . yer just float around polishin' stars . . . checking out Mars an' that. Hangin' off Orion's belt. (*Pause.*) Either that or I reckon I might just wanna come here. I think. Do what we do but without goin' back to all the crap . . . all the reponsibility. Just sitting off with a bevvy, drawin' in the sunshine cos it wouldn't rain.

CHRISTIE. Sounds alright.

LUKE. I think about it.

Pause.

CHRISTIE. I want yer to know –

LUKE. I know, yeah.

CHRISTIE. I haven't said anythin' yet.

LUKE. But I know – Not . . . being funny or nothing, it's just . . . don't wanna go through all that. Not really what I came for.

CHRISTIE. Alright.

LUKE. I get pains behind my eyes.

Pause.

CHRISTIE. I wanna –

LUKE. I feel . . . older, but not in a good way. I don't feel
mature or owt. Wise. I just feel . . . old.

CHRISTIE. I am here, y'know . . . I just wanna sit an' talk ab–

LUKE. I've sat with yer . . . in me head . . . in the dark . . . for
days, weeks on end. Listened to yer, the same words over
and over . . . telling me about wantin' to change the world,
tryin' not to preach and preachin' at the same time, like I
won't notice . . . like there's anythin' I can do fuckin'
anyway . . . everythin' around me's gettin' destroyed and
I'm so fuckin' . . . jealous of yer. I wish I had someone to
send me thoughts to. Sat in a bedroom, safe as houses with
yer tape recorder, talking sense to someone who feels
completely fuckin' mad. Until yer decide there's no point
trying to talk sense to someone so different. And sometimes
I think yer right and sometimes I think yer wrong. I think
we've pretty much got the same stuff in our heads, Chris. I
just hate the way you never asked what mine was.

Pause.

CHRISTIE. I'm sor–

LUKE. I did yer somethin'.

*He rummages about in his bag then brings out a small
canvas, he looks at it for a second or so before handing it
over.* CHRISTIE *studies it.*

CHRISTIE. It's sound, that. Nice one.

LUKE. Ta.

CHRISTIE. What is it?

LUKE. Dunno.

CHRISTIE. Could be me and you.

LUKE. Could be, yeah.

CHRISTIE. Thanks, Luke.

LUKE. S'alright. Tried to do one of when yer were born . . .
like yer told me about . . . you lying there, next to the road,
lookin' up at the sky. Was shit though. Decided I'm better at
just seein' what happens. Chuckin' a bit o' paint on and
makin' a shape I like.

Pause.

CHRISTIE. Brought the fishin' rods.

LUKE. Can't stay really . . . not for much longer.

CHRISTIE. Right. I thought –

LUKE. Need to see me mam. She's gone all hectic on me.
Tries to tuck me in an' everythin' . . . said I'd get back for
me tea.

CHRISTIE. Could walk back with yer?

LUKE. Nah, yer alright. Just gonna run.

LUKE *stands and* CHRISTIE *follows. They stand awkwardly,
sort of facing each other, not quite sure what to do.*

CHRISTIE. Thanks. For me picture.

LUKE. S'OK.

CHRISTIE. I'm gonna put it above me bed.

Pause.

LUKE. Better had get goin'.

Pause.

CHRISTIE. Give yer a call or somethin'.

LUKE. Yeah.

CHRISTIE. See yer again soon.

LUKE. See yer, Chris.

LUKE *leaves and* CHRISTIE *watches him go until he's out
of sight. He sits down and picks the picture up.*

End.